DATE DUE

DEMCO 38-296

KECKEIS

The Black
Rose

Die
Schwarze
Rose

La Rose
Noire

La Rosa
Negra

PRO LINGUA PRESS

First Edition

ISBN No. 1-879870-54-1

Manufactured in the United States of America.

Published by Pro Lingua Press, Los Angeles, California

Illustrations: Christophe Cassidy

Translations: Frank Steiner
                   Dennis Mercer
                   Anne Beaubeau
                   Louis Fernandez

Dust Cover
Title Page: Evelyne Bermann

Index

The Little Star	La Petite Etoile
Der Kleine Stern	La Pequeña Estrella

Twilight spread over the sky like an enormous blanket. Workers laid down their tools, the hammer, the pencil, the brush, and turned off all the machines they had kept running all day long.

Quitting time... They went home or to the park, the beach or to the quiet streets of the big city. Up in the sky, the first stars began to twinkle brightly, glistening like jewels set against black velvet.

"Do you see that little star over there in the handle of the Big Dipper? That's where I will meet my mother when

★★★

Wie eine riesige Decke breitete die Dämmerung sich über den Himmel aus. Arbeiter legten ihr Werkzeug aus der Hand, den Hammer, den Bleistift, den Pinsel, und drehten die Maschinen ab, die sie den ganzen Tag über in Trab gehalten hatten.

Feierabend...Sie gingen heim oder in den Park, an den Strand oder durch die nun ruhigen Gassen der grossen Stadt. Oben am Himmel begannen die ersten Sterne hell zu blinken, glitzernd wie Edelsteine auf schwarzem Samt.

"Siehst du den kleinen Stern, dort, an der Deichsel des grossen Wagens? Dort will ich mich mit meiner Mut-

Le crépuscule recouvrit le ciel comme un immense manteau. Les ouvriers posèrent leurs outils, marteau, crayon, brosse, et stoppèrent les machines qu'ils avaient fait marcher toute la journée.

C'était l'heure de quitter le travail pour la journée. Ils s'en allèrent vers leurs foyers, vers le parc, la plage, ou les rues tranquilles de la grande ville. Là-haut, dans le ciel, les premières étoiles se mirent à scintiller vivement, comme des joyaux sur du velours noir.

«Tu vois cette petite étoile, là-bas, sur la queue de la Grande Ourse? C'est là que je retrouverai ma mère quand

★ ★

El crepúsculo se extendió sobre el cielo como una enorme manta. Los trabajadores pusieron a un lado sus herramientas, el martillo, el lápiz, la brocha, y apagaron las máquinas que habían tenido andando todo el día.

Hora de cesar. . . Se fueron a casa o al parque, a la playa o a las tranquilas calles de la gran ciudad. Arriba en el cielo, las primeras estrellas empezaron a destellar brillantemente, reluciendo como joyas contra un fondo de terciopelo negro.

—¿Ves esa pequeña estrella allá en la manija del Gran Carro? Ahí es donde encontraré a mi madre cuando yo

I die," a woman told her small son, and the boy peered up eagerly, hoping to see his grandmother sitting there, waiting, perhaps even waving down at him.

"I, too, would like to be looked at," murmured a tiny star suspended high up in the sky. "I, too, would like to be chosen to be a meeting place, or as a lead star for fishermen, or for some other important purpose like that." And he brushed his shoes and polished his belt buckle extra hard so he would shine more brightly than the other stars.

★ ★

ter treffen, wenn ich einmal sterbe", sagte eine Frau zu ihrem kleinen Sohn. Der Bub starrte angestrengt hinauf, um vielleicht seine Grossmutter zu erblicken, wie sie dort oben sass und wartete und vielleicht sogar zu ihm herunterwinkte.

"Ich möchte auch so beachtet werden", murmelte ein winziger Stern, der hoch oben am Himmel hing. "Ich möchte auch als Treffpunkt ausgesucht werden oder als Leitstern für die Fischer oder für eine andere bedeutende Aufgabe." Angestrengt wichste er seine Schuhe und polierte seine Gürtelschnalle, um heller zu leuchten als die anderen Sterne.

je serai morte» dit une dame à son jeune fils; alors l'enfant scruta le ciel avidement, espérant voir sa grand-mère assise là-haut, à attendre, et peut-être même à lui faire signe.

«Moi aussi, j'aimerais qu'on me regarde», murmura une toute petite étoile suspendue là-haut dans le ciel. «Moi aussi, j'aimerais qu'on me choisisse comme lieu de rendez-vous, ou pour guider les pêcheurs, ou pour quelque autre tâche aussi importante!» Elle astiqua ses souliers et polit la boucle de sa ceinture encore plus fort, pour briller avec plus d'éclat que les autres étoiles.

★★★★★★★★★★★★★★★★★★★★★★★★★★★★★★★★★★★★★★★

muera —dijo una mujer a su pequeño hijo, y el chico miró hacia arriba afanosamente, con la ilusión de ver a su abuela sentada, esperando, quizás saludándola inclusive.

—A mí también me gustaría que me miraran —murmuró una diminuta estrella suspendida en lo alto del cielo.

—A mí también me gustaría ser escogida para ser un punto de reunión, o como estrella guía para los pescadores, o para algún otro fin igualmente importante—. Y cepilló sus zapatos y pulió la hebilla de su cinturón con energía extraordinaria para poder brillar más resplandeciente-mente que las otras estrellas.

"Such a vain fellow," the star next to him said disapprovingly, and another star chided, "You don't become a lead star overnight. You have to grow up and do your job well, year in and year out, whether you are being watched or not, recognized or not—and not for the rewards, but because it is your duty. Only then," he said, "will you begin to glow so strong and steadily that the fishermen will trust you and guide their boats by your light, but that will take many millions of nights."

"Many millions of nights!" The little star thrust out his lower lip defiantly. "Who has that much time?" Then

★ ★

"So ein eitler Kerl", ärgerte sich der Stern neben ihm, und ein anderer meinte: "Zum Leitstern wirst du nicht von heute auf morgen. Dazu musst du wachsen und deine Aufgabe erfüllen, jahraus, jahrein, beachtet oder unbeachtet, anerkannt oder unerkannt, und nicht um der Belohnung willen, sondern deshalb, weil es deine Pflicht ist. Nur dann", fuhr er fort, "wirst du so stark zu leuchten beginnen, dass die Fischer sich trauen können, ihre Boote nach deinem Schein zu steuern; doch das dauert viele Millionen Nächte."

"Viele Millionen Nächte", wiederholte der kleine Stern und schob trotzig seine Unterlippe vor. "Wer hat

14

«Quelle consœur prétentieuse!» dit l'étoile voisine d'un ton désapprobateur, et une autre étoile la réprimanda: «On ne devient pas une étoile qui peut servir de guide du jour au lendemain. Il faut que tu grandisses et que tu fasses bien ton travail, année après année, que l'on t'observe ou pas, que l'on te reconnaisse ou pas, non pour les récompenses mais parce que c'est ton devoir. Alors seulement, dit-elle, tu commenceras à briller tellement fort que les pêcheurs se fieront à toi et guideront leurs bateaux d'après ta lumière, mais cela prendra plusieurs millions de nuits.»

«Plusieurs millions de nuits!» répéta la petite étoile, et elle fit une moue de défi: «Je ne peux pas attendre si long-

★★

—¡Qué compañera tan vana! —dijo la estrella vecina con desaprobación—. Y otra estrella refunfuñó: —No puedes estar a la cabeza de las estrellas de la noche a la mañana. Tienes que crecer y desempeñar bien tu trabajo, año tras año, ya bien seas observada o no, reconocida o no, y no por las recompensas, sino porque ése es tu deber. Sólo entonces —dijo—, empezarás a brillar tan intensamente que los pescadores confiarán en ti y guiarán sus botes mediante tu luz, pero esto tomará muchos millones de noches.

—¡Muchos millones de noches! —repitió la pequeña estrella y sacó con fuerza su labio inferior desafiante.

15

he smoothed his silvery cloak and began to wiggle his legs so that perhaps someone down on Earth would notice him.

"Maybe I should get down a bit closer so the people on Earth can see me more easily," he thought, and with his little fingers he carefully undid the knot that held him to the sky and started to climb down cautiously. Then firmly grasping the rope, for he was very afraid to fall, he swayed back and forth until his silvery cape was fluttering in the wind.

★★★★★★★★★★★★★★★★★★★★★★★★★★★★★★★★★★★★★★★

denn so lange Zeit?" Dann glättete er seinen silbernen Mantel und schlenkerte mit den Beinen, um vielleicht doch von jemandem auf Erden wahrgenommen zu werden.

"Möglicherweise sollte ich etwas tiefer hängen, so dass die Menschen auf der Erde mich leichter sehen können", überlegte er. Mit seinen kleinen Fingern löste er vorsichtig den Knoten des Seils, das ihn am Himmel festhielt und kletterte behutsam tiefer. Fest umklammerte er das Seil, denn er hatte grosse Angst hinunterzufallen, und schwang dabei hin und her, bis sein silberner Umhang im Wind flatterte.

temps!» Elle lissa alors sa cape argentée et se mit à agiter les jambes, en espérant que quelqu'un sur Terre la remarquerait.

«Peut-être devrais-je descendre un peu plus près pour que les gens sur la Terre me voient plus facilement», pensa-t-elle. De ses petits doigts, elle défit précautionneusement le nœud de la corde qui la retenait au ciel, et se mit à descendre prudemment. Puis, agrippant fermement la corde, car elle avait très peur de tomber, elle se balança d'avant en arrière jusqu'à ce que sa cape d'argent flottât dans le vent.

★★★

—¿Quién posee todo este tiempo?—Entonces suavizó su manto plateado y comenzó a menear sus piernas con la esperanza de que alguien abajo en La Tierra la notara.

—Quizás deba bajar un poco más cerca de modo que la gente de La Tierra me pueda ver con mayor facilidad —pensó—. Con sus pequeños dedos desató cuidadosamente el nudo de la soga que la sostenía desde el cielo y empezó a descender con precaución.

Entonces, asiendo la soga firmemente, pues tenía un gran temor de caer, se columpió hacia delante y hacia atrás hasta que su capa plateada comenzó a ondular estrepitosamente en el aire.

17

But no one seemed to look up at him.

"Why doesn't anyone notice me?" he lamented and reached out, waving one hand. Then it dawned on him, "Perhaps I am still too high up." And he lowered himself a little more. Before long, he had reached the bottom of the rope and was holding on only with his arms while he kicked his legs crazily to keep the rope swaying.

"People have to see me now, they have to see me!" he shouted into the night and also began shaking his arm. Now he was holding onto the rope with just one hand while he rocked back and forth wildly.

★★★★★★★★★★★★★★★★★★★★★★★★★★★★★★★★★★★★★★

Doch niemand schien zu ihm heraufzublicken.

"Warum bemerkt mich denn niemand?" jammerte er und streckte seine Hand aus, um zu winken. "Vielleicht bin ich immer noch zu hoch oben", dachte er und kletterte noch ein Stückchen tiefer. Schliesslich war er am Ende des Seils angelangt und hielt sich nur noch mit den Armen fest, während die Beine wild herumstrampelten, um das Seil in Schwung zu halten.

"Die Menschen müssen mich nun sehen, sie müssen mich sehen!" rief er in die Nacht hinein, während er mit einem Arm winkte. Nun hielt er sich gar nur noch mit einer Hand am Seil fest und schaukelte wild hin und her.

Mais personne ne semblait la remarquer.

«Comment se fait-il que personne ne me remarque?» se lamenta-t-elle, tendant le bras pour faire des signes. «Peut-être suis-je encore trop haut», se dit-elle, et elle descendit davantage. Bien vite, elle eut atteint le bout de la corde et n'était plus suspendue que par les bras, battant frénétiquement des jambes pour que la corde continue à se balancer.

«On doit me voir maintenant, on doit me voir!» s'écriat-elle dans la nuit en agitant le bras. Elle ne se cramponnait à la corde que d'une main tout en se balançant frénétiquement d'avant en arrière.

* *

Pero nadie parecía voltear hacia arriba para verle.

—¿Porqué nadie me nota? —se lamentó estirando hacia el frente su mano—. Tal vez estoy muy en alto todavía —se le ocurrió y bajó un poco más—. Pronto, había ya alcanzado el final de la soga sosteniéndose solamente con los brazos mientras pataleaba alocadamente para que la soga siguiese oscilando.

—La gente tiene que verme ahora, tiene que verme! —gritó a la noche sacudiendo a la vez, su brazo—. Ahora se estaba sujetando de la soga solamente con una mano mientras se mecía frenéticamente hacia adelante y hacia atrás.

No one knows exactly what happened after that but suddenly the nearby stars saw the empty rope swinging in the wind like the rope pull at the end of a heavy church bell that has just been started.

Meanwhile, the little star was paralyzed with fright as he plunged through space toward the Earth. He spread out his arms like a bird attempting to fly for the very first time. As the steep dive caused his hair and clothes to flutter in the wind, a long, silver streak suddenly became visible across the dark sky.

★★

Niemand weiss genau, was dann geschah, doch plötzlich sahen die umliegenden Sterne das leere Seil im Wind hin und her pendeln wie den Seilzug einer schweren Turmglocke, die man soeben in Gang gesetzt hatte.

Der kleine Stern jedoch war starr vor Entsetzen, als er spürte, dass er ins Bodenlose stürzte. Er breitete seine Arme aus wie ein Vogel, der das erste Mal zu fliegen versucht. Der Sturzflug liess seine Haare und Kleider im Wind flattern, so dass ein langer, silberner Streifen sich über den dunklen Himmel zog.

Personne ne sait exactement ce qui arriva ensuite, mais tout à coup, les étoiles voisines virent la corde libre osciller dans le vent telle l'extrémité de la corde d'une lourde cloche d'église qu'on vient de mettre en branle.

Pendant ce temps-là, la petite étoile était paralysée de frayeur tandis qu'elle plongeait à travers l'espace en direction de la Terre. Elle ouvrit les bras comme un oiseau qui essaye de voler pour la première fois. La brusque descente fit voler sa chevelure et son costume dans le vent et une longue traînée argentée apparut soudain dans le ciel obscur.

★★★

Nadie sabe exactamente qué pasó después de esto pero repentinamente las estrellas vecinas vieron la soga vacía oscilando en el viento como el tirón de una soga al extremo de una pesada campana de iglesia que acaba de ser tocada.

Entre tanto, la pequeña estrella estaba paralizada de susto mientras se precipitaba a través del espacio en dirección a La Tierra. Extendió sus brazos como un pájaro que intenta volar por primera vez. Ya que la precipitada caída hacía que su cabello y vestido se batieran agitadamente en el viento, pronto se hizo visible un rayo largo y plateado a través del oscuro cielo.

"Look, a shooting star!" cried the mother, hugging her little boy close to her. "Quick, make a wish—and it will be granted." In the park, on the beach and along the quiet streets of the big city, people stopped to look up in awe at the flight of the shooting star. Just as instantly, their wishes rose skyward toward the heavens, large ones and small ones, red ones and white ones, and bright green ones with pink dots. Wishes of all colors, shapes and sizes floated up toward the little star, and his hands outstretched in flight grasped all they could catch.

★★★★★★★★★★★★★★★★★★★★★★★★★★★★★★★★★★★★★

"Schau, eine Sternschnuppe!" rief die Mutter aus und hielt den kleinen Jungen fest umarmt. "Schnell, wünsch dir etwas, und es wird in Erfüllung gehen." Im Park, am Strand und in den stillen Strassen der grossen Stadt hielten die Menschen inne und blickten andächtig dem Flug der Sternschnuppe nach. Zugleich stiegen ihre Wünsche hinauf zum Himmel, grosse und kleine, rote und weisse, und hellgrüne mit rosa Punkten. Wünsche in allen Farben, Formen und Grössen schwebten dem kleinen Stern entgegen, und seine ausgestreckten Hände ergriffen im Vorbeiflug so viele sie nur fangen konnten.

24

«Regarde, une étoile filante!» s'écria la mère en serrant contre elle son petit garçon. «Vite, fais un vœu, et il sera exaucé.»

Dans le parc, sur la plage, et le long des rues tranquilles de la grande ville, les gens s'arrêtaient pour regarder dans le ciel, subjugués, la trajectoire de l'étoile filante. Presque instantanément, leurs vœux s'élevèrent vers les cieux, les grands et les petits, les rouges et le blancs, ainsi que les verts brillants à pois roses. Des vœux de toutes couleurs, de toutes formes et de toutes tailles s'envolèrent vers la petite étoile, et ses mains tendues dans le vol saisirent tous ceux qu'elle pouvait attraper.

★★★★★★★★★★★★★★★★★★★★★★★★★★★★★★★★★★★★★★★

—¡Mira, una estrella fugaz! —dijo la madre, abrazando fuertemente a su pequeño niño—. Pronto, pide un deseo, y te será concedido.

En el parque, en la playa y en las tranquilas calles de la gran ciudad, la gente se detuvo a mirar hacia arriba, impresionada por el vuelo de la estrella fugaz. Igualmente rápido, sus deseos se elevaron al cielo, grandes y pequeños, rojos y blancos, verdes con puntos rosados. Deseos de todos colores, formas y tamaños se elevaron hacia la pequeña estrella, y sus manos extendidas en vuelo cogieron cuanto pudieron atrapar.

The little star held up the wishes like two big bunches of balloons, and to his amazement suddenly noticed that his free-fall through space was slowing down. More and more wishes soared up to meet him and he grabbed every-one of them. Slowly, he began to rise again, borne by the power of the countless hopes he held clutched in his hands.

Just then, the words of the wise, older star re-echoed in his ears: "You have to do your job—not for the rewards, but because it is your duty. . .", and he kept looking for wishes that had gone astray in space so he could collect

★ ★

Der kleine Stern hielt die Wünsche fest, wie zwei Bouquets von Luftballons, und merkte plötzlich mit Verwunderung, dass sich sein Flug durchs Weltall verlangsamte. Mehr und mehr Wünsche kamen ihm entgegen und er ergriff jeden einzelnen. Langsam begann er wieder aufzusteigen, getragen von der Kraft der unzähligen Hoffnungen, die er in Händen hielt.

Ihm fielen die Worte des alten, weisen Sterns wieder ein: "Du musst deine Aufgabe erfüllen, nicht um des Erfolges willen, sondern weil es deine Pflicht ist...", und er hielt Ausschau nach verirrten Wünschen, die im All

La petite étoile tenait les vœux comme deux grosses gerbes de ballons, et à sa grande surprise, elle remarqua que sa chute libre à travers l'espace se ralentissait. Des vœux de plus en plus nombreux montaient à sa rencontre, et elle les attrapait tous. Doucement, elle se mit à remonter, portée par la puissance des espoirs innombrables qu'elle tenait serrés dans ses mains.

C'est alors que les propos de la vieille et sage étoile lui revinrent en tête: «Tu dois faire ton travail, non pas pour les récompenses, mais parce que c'est ton devoir...», et elle continua à chercher les vœux qui s'étaient égarés dans

★★★

La pequeña estrella sostuvo los deseos como dos grandes manojos de globos, y, con sorpresa, repentinamente se percató de que su caída libre a través del espacio se empezaba a detener. Más y más deseos se elevaban para alcanzarle, y ella los tomaba uno tras otro. Lentamente, empezó a elevarse de nuevo, propulsada por el poder de los incontables anhelos que había atrapado en sus manos.

Justo entonces, las palabras de la vieja, sabia estrella resonaron en sus oídos: «Tienes que hacer tu trabajo, no por las recompensas, sino porque es tu deber.» Y continuó buscando los deseos que se habían extraviado en el espacio

them and take them to the source where all wishes are fulfilled.

The little star felt happier than he ever could remember. He had a task, an extremely important task. And he wanted nothing more now than to float around in space and gather up each and every wish. Being noticed or recognized no longer seemed to matter. In his little silver breast, he suddenly felt a warming glow, and a small, gleaming halo brightened the night all around him.

★★

umherflogen, um sie einzusammeln und dorthin zu bringen, wo alle Wünsche in Erfüllung gehen.

Der kleine Stern war glücklich wie nie zuvor. Er hatte eine Aufgabe, eine überaus wichtige Aufgabe. Er wollte im All nach Wünschen suchen und jeden einzelnen einsammeln. Beachtet oder anerkannt zu werden, schien ihm mit einem Mal nicht mehr so wichtig. In seiner engen, silbernen Brust aber spürte er plötzlich eine seltsame Wärme, und ein kleiner Strahlenkranz erhellte die Nacht um ihn herum.

l'espace pour les recueillir et les emporter vers la source où tous les vœux sont comblés.

La petite étoile se sentit heureuse comme jamais elle ne l'avait été. Elle avait une tâche, une tâche extrêmement importante. Elle ne souhaitait maintenant rien d'autre que de voler dans l'espace pour rassembler tous les vœux. Etre remarquée ou reconnue semblait ne plus lui être d'aucune importance. Dans son petit cœur d'argent, elle sentit soudain une chaleur ardente, et un petit halo lumineux éclaira la nuit tout autour d'elle.

★★★★★★★★★★★★★★★★★★★★★★★★★★★★★★★★★★

para poder recogerlos y llevarlos a la fuente donde todos los anhelos se cumplen.

La pequeña estrella se sintió más feliz que nunca. Tenía una tarea, una tarea extremadamente importante. Y ahora no quería nada más que flotar en el espacio para recoger todos y cada uno de los deseos. El ser notada o reconocida ya no le parecía ser importante. En su estrecho pecho plateado, repentinamente sintió un cálido resplandor, y un pequeño y fulgurante halo iluminó la noche todo a su alrededor.

31

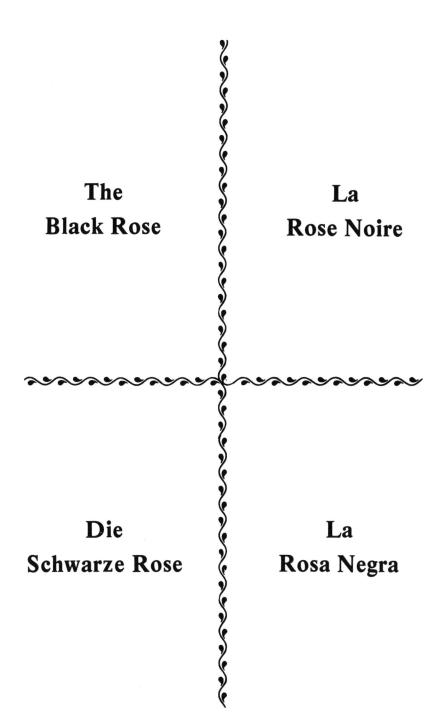

The
Black Rose

La
Rose Noire

Die
Schwarze Rose

La
Rosa Negra

In a small country village, somewhere in this big, wide world, lived two young people who liked one another. They were both very poor, like everyone else in their village, but it did not bother them. Nature had endowed the girl with great beauty and the young man possessed a very special gift. With his hands he was able to grow the most beautiful flowers, the most prolific trees and bountiful gardens.

They soon got married and moved into a cottage at the edge of the village. The young man worked at his job from

In einem kleinen Dorf, irgendwo auf dieser grossen, weiten Welt, lebten zwei junge Menschen, die aneinander Gefallen fanden. Sie waren beide sehr arm, doch jeder in ihrem Dorf war so arm, deshalb störte es sie nicht weiter. Ausserdem hatte die Natur das Mädchen mit grosser Schönheit ausgestattet. Der Bursche aber besass eine besondere Gabe. Seine Hände konnten die schönsten Blumen, die ertragreichsten Bäume und die fruchtbarsten Gärten züchten.

Die beiden heirateten und bezogen ein kleines Haus am Rand des Dorfes. Der junge Mann ging von früh bis

Dans un petit village, quelque part dans ce vaste monde, vivaient deux jeunes gens qui s'aimaient. Tous deux étaient très pauvres, mais tout le monde l'était dans le village, par conséquent cela ne les dérangeait pas. En outre, la nature avait doté la jeune fille d'une grande beauté. Le jeune homme, quant à lui, possédait un don spécial. De ses mains, il pouvait faire pousser les fleurs les plus belles, les arbres les plus prolifiques et les jardins les plus luxuriants.

Bientôt, ils se marièrent et s'installèrent dans une petite maison à la lisière du village. Le jeune homme travaillait

En una pequeña aldea, en alguna parte de este grande y ancho mundo, vivían dos jóvenes que se querían. Ambos eran muy pobres, pero todos los demás en su pueblo lo eran también, así que eso no les preocupaba. Además, la naturaleza había dotado a la muchacha de gran hermosura y el joven poseía un don muy especial. Con sus manos, era capaz de cultivar las flores más hermosas, los más prolíficos árboles y los jardines más generosos.

Pronto se casaron y se mudaron a una pequeña cabaña a la orilla del pueblo. El joven laboraba desde el amanecer

dawn to dusk, yet when he returned home he never failed to kneel down in his garden and plant the most gorgeous flowers.

In the morning, before he left for work, he would go out to the garden and cut the brightest blossoms for his young wife. For a while all of this pleased her very much.

People often stopped in front of their neat little house to admire the magnificent flowers. The woman was delighted when she peeked out from behind the curtains and saw their admiration.

spät seiner Arbeit nach. Doch wenn er heimkehrte, verabsäumte er es nie, in seinem Garten niederzuknien und die wundervollsten Gewächse zu pflanzen.

Morgens bevor er zur Arbeit aufbrach, ging er in den Garten und schnitt die schönsten Blumen für seine junge Frau. Eine Zeitlang gefiel ihr all das sehr gut.

Die Leute blieben oft vor ihrem sauberen, kleinen Haus stehen, um die herrlichen Blumen zu bewundern. Wenn die Frau dann zwischen den Vorhängen hinausspähte und die anerkennenden Blicke sah, so freute sie dies sehr.

du matin au soir. Pourtant, lorsqu'il rentrait chez lui, il ne manquait jamais de s'agenouiller dans son jardin pour y planter les fleurs les plus ravissantes qu'il pût trouver.

Le matin, avant de partir pour le travail, il allait de nouveau au jardin pour cueillir les fleurs les plus éclatantes pour sa jeune femme. Pendant quelque temps, elle fut enchantée de tout cela.

Des gens s'arrêtaient souvent devant la jolie petite maison pour admirer les fleurs magnifiques. Quand la femme jetait un œil entre les rideaux, voyant leur expression emerveillée, elle était ravie.

hasta el anochecer. Aun así, al regresar a casa jamás dejaba de arrodillarse en su jardín para plantar las más hermosas flores.

Por la mañana, antes de salir a trabajar, él salía al jardín y cortaba las más esplendorosas flores para su joven esposa. Esto la complació mucho durante un tiempo. A menudo la gente se detenía enfrente de su pulcra casita para admirar las magníficas flores. La mujer quedaba complacida cuando atisbaba de detrás de las cortinas y veía sus miradas de asombro.

In time, though, she grew tired of the poor villagers' admiration. And, she had heard talk about the small town nearby with its fine department stores and shops and the exciting bustle of the marketplace.

The very next morning, when her husband came in with an armful of fresh flowers for her, she angrily shoved them aside.

"I am tired of this village," she said. "I am tired of your flowers. Go get us a house in town!"

Doch mit der Zeit wurde ihr die Bewunderung der armen Dörfler langweilig. Auch hatte sie von der nahegelegenen, kleinen Stadt gehört, von den schönen Kaufhäusern und Geschäften und dem bunten Treiben auf dem Marktplatz.

Am nächsten Morgen, als ihr Mann wieder mit einem Arm voll frischer Blumen eintrat, da schob die Frau den Strauss verärgert zur Seite.

"Mich langweilt das Dorfleben", sagte sie. "Mich langweilen deine Blumen. Geh und schaff uns ein Haus in der Stadt!"

Un jour, pourtant, elle se lassa de l'admiration des pauvres campagnards. D'autre part, elle avait entendu parler du bourg voisin, avec ses grands magasins, ses boutiques, et l'animation excitante de la place du marché.

Dès le lendemain matin, lorsque son mari rentra dans la maison avec une pleine brassée de fleurs fraîches, elle les repoussa avec humeur.

«Je suis lasse de la vie dans ce village!» dit-elle. «Je suis lasse de tes fleurs. Va nous trouver une maison en ville!»

Con el tiempo, sin embargo, se cansó de la admiración de los pobres aldeanos. Además, había oído hablar de la pequeña ciudad cercana, de sus finas tiendas de departamentos y almacenes, y del efervescente pulular del mercado.

La mañana siguiente, cuando el esposo entró con un manojo de flores frescas, la esposa las aventó a un lado con enojo.

—Estoy cansada de este pueblo —dijo ella—. Estoy cansada de tus flores. ¡Ve a conseguirnos una casa en la ciudad!

Sadly the man put down the flowers and set out for town to look for a house.

It was not easy to find the right place. Most of the small, gray houses stood close together in long rows, leaving almost no room for flowers or shrubs. He finally found a house on the outskirts of town, surrounded by a small yard. He knelt down right away and planted some colorful bushes and hedges. Then he drove back to fetch his wife.

Da legte der Mann die Blumen traurig zur Seite und ging in die Stadt, um ein Haus zu suchen.

Es war gar nicht leicht, den richtigen Platz zu finden, denn die meisten der kleinen, grauen Häuser standen eng aneinandergereiht in langen Strassenzügen und liessen kaum Raum für Blumen oder Sträucher. Am Rand der Stadt fand er endlich ein Haus, umgeben von einem kleinen Garten, das er erwarb. Sofort kniete er nieder und pflanzte ein paar bunte Sträucher und Hecken. Dann fuhr er zurück, um seine Frau zu holen.

Tristement, l'homme posa les fleurs et partit en ville chercher une maison.

Il ne lui fut pas facile de trouver l'endroit parfait car la plupart des petites maisons grises étaient très proches les unes des autres, disposées en longues rangées, sans presque aucun espace pour une fleur ou un arbuste. Finalement, il trouva dans un faubourg une maison entourée d'un petit jardin et l'acheta. Il s'agenouilla tout de suite pour planter des haies et des massifs de couleurs vives. Puis il retourna chercher sa femme.

Tristemente, el hombre dejó a un lado las flores y se dirigió a la ciudad para buscar una casa.

No era fácil encontrar el lugar apropiado pues la mayoría de las casas pequeñas y grises estaban juntas en largas hileras, y no dejaban prácticamente ningún espacio para las flores o los follajes. Finalmente, en las afueras de la ciudad encontró una casa rodeada por un pequeño terreno, y la adquirió. Se hincó inmediatamente y plantó algunos arbustos y setos llenos de color. Enseguida regresó a la aldea para buscar a su esposa y llevarla a su nuevo hogar.

When they arrived at their new home, the whole garden was radiantly in bloom.

People passing by stopped to admire the garden because such a display of beauty was truly a rare sight.

Before long, the man was very busy. Everyone in town asked him for advice. Someone had a balcony which he wanted to fill with flowering plants, another had a small yard he wanted to turn into a garden. With his magic touch, the young man soon had the window sills of all the

Als sie in ihrem neuen Heim ankamen, da stand der ganze Garten schon in voller Blüte.

Die vorbeikommenden Leute blieben voll Bewunderung stehen, denn der Anblick solcher Schönheit war ein wahrhaft seltenes Bild.

Bald hatte der Mann alle Hände voll zu tun. Jedermann in der Stadt bat ihn um Rat. Der eine hatte einen Balkon, den er mit blühenden Pflanzen füllen wollte, ein anderer besass einen kleinen Hof, den er in einen Garten zu verwandeln suchte. Der junge Mann zauberte Blüten

Quand ils arrivèrent à leur nouveau foyer, le jardin tout entier regorgeait de fleurs. Les passants s'arrêtaient pour l'admirer car un tel étalage de beauté était un spectacle rare.

L'homme fut vite très occupé. Tout le monde lui demandait conseil. L'un avait un balcon qu'il voulait couvrir de plantes fleuries, un autre avait un petit bout de terrain qu'il souhaitait transformer en jardin. Par son toucher magique, le jeune homme fit apparaître une abondante floraison sur le rebord des fenêtres de toutes les

Cuando llegaron a su nueva casa, el jardín entero estaba floreciendo radiantemente.

La gente que pasaba por ahí se detenía a admirarlo porque tal despliegue de belleza era un espectáculo poco común.

Después de poco tiempo el hombre se vio lleno de trabajo. Todo el mundo en la ciudad le pedía consejos. Uno tenía una terraza que quería llenar de flores, otra tenía un pequeño patio que anhelaba convertir en jardín. Con su toque mágico, el joven pronto hizo florecer las re-

gray houses in full bloom. In the middle of the town square he planted a huge oak tree where the townspeople could sit and chat in its shade.

Meanwhile, his wife went shopping at the fine stores and bought new hats and dresses. When she returned home, she always found some fresh flowers, for her husband brought her a new bouquet every day.

For a while all of this pleased her very much. Then one day she saw pictures of the great capital city of their

auf die Fenstersimse der grauen Häuser, und mitten auf dem Marktplatz pflanzte er eine grosse Eiche, in deren Schatten die Leute sitzen und plaudern konnten.

Die Frau besuchte inzwischen die schönen Geschäfte und kaufte sich neue Hüte und Kleider. Kehrte sie dann heim, so fand sie immer frische Blumen vor, denn der Mann brachte ihr täglich einen frischen Strauss.

Eine Zeitlang gefiel ihr all das sehr gut. Doch eines Tages sah sie Bilder der grossen Hauptstadt ihres Landes,

maisons grises et, au milieu du square de la ville, il planta un immense chêne, à l'ombre duquel les citadins pouvaient venir s'asseoir et bavarder.

Sa femme, quant à elle, allait voir les beaux magasins et acheter de nouveaux chapeaux et de nouvelles robes. Quand elle rentrait à la maison, elle trouvait toujours un arrangement de fleurs fraîches, car son mari lui apportait un nouveau bouquet tous les jours.

Pendant quelque temps, elle en fut enchantée. Puis un jour, elle vit des images de la grande capitale, où vivaient le

pisas de las ventanas en todas las casas grises, y en medio de la plaza de la ciudad plantó un enorme roble donde los vecinos podían sentarse y conversar bajo su sombra.

Su esposa, mientras tanto, iba de compras a las tiendas finas y compraba sombreros y vestidos nuevos. Al regresar a casa, siempre encontraba arreglos de flores frescas, porque su marido le traía un ramo nuevo diariamente.

Esto la satisfizo durante un tiempo. Pero después, un día, ella vio fotografías de la gran capital de su país en el

country, where the king lived with his ministers. She saw pictures of the lavish royal receptions, of ladies in flowing evening gowns wearing sparkling jewelry.

That day, when her husband came in with an armful of fresh flowers, she shoved them aside angrily.

"I am tired of this small town life," she said. "I am tired of your flowers. Go get us a house in the capital where the king lives."

Hearing this, the husband grew very sad. He liked the

wo der König mit seinen Ministern lebte. Sie sah Bilder von den prunkvollen königlichen Empfängen, von Damen in fliessenden Abendkleidern mit ihrem glitzernden Schmuck.

Als ihr Mann an diesem Tag wieder mit einem Arm voll frischer Blumen hereinkam, da schob die Frau den Strauss verärgert zur Seite.

"Mich langweilt das Kleinstadtleben", sagte sie. "Mich langweilen deine Blumen. Geh und schaff uns ein Haus in der Hauptstadt, dort wo der König lebt."

Als er das hörte, wurde der Mann sehr traurig. Er

roi et ses ministres. Elle vit des images des somptueuses réceptions royales, des dames en longues robes de soirée, couvertes de bijoux étincelants.

Lorsque son mari rentra ce jour-là avec une brassée de fleurs fraîches, elle les repoussa avec humeur.

«Je suis lasse de cette vie dans ce bourg!» dit-elle. «Je suis lasse de tes fleurs. Va nous trouver une maison dans la capitale, là où habite le roi.»

A ces mots, le mari fut très attristé. Il aimait la petite

que el rey vivía con sus ministros. Ella vio fotografías de las suntuosas recepciones reales y de damas con ondulantes vestidos de gala luciendo joyería esplendorosa.

Cuando su esposo entró ese día con un manojo de flores frescas, la esposa airadamente las hizo a un lado.

—Estoy cansada de esta vida, pueblerina —dijo—. Estoy cansada de tus flores. !Consíguenos una casa en la capital, donde vive el rey!

Al oír esto, el esposo se entristeció. Le gustaba este

little town that he had saved from its eternal grayness. He liked the people too. But he wanted to grant his wife's wishes, for he loved her very much.

The next day he traveled to the big city, with its fine buildings, its luxury and excitement, but with all its noise and dust too. He soon found a magnificent palace with broad white marble steps leading from the terrace into an adjoining park. He immediately set to work. It took him several days to bring everything he had planted into bloom.

mochte die kleine Stadt, die er von ihrem ewigen Grau erlöst hatte. Er mochte auch die Leute. Doch wollte er seiner Frau jeden Wunsch erfüllen, denn er liebte sie sehr.

Tags darauf fuhr er in die grosse Stadt mit all den schönen Bauten, mit all ihrem Luxus und Trubel, aber auch mit all ihrem Lärm und Staub. Er fand ein prächtiges Palais, von dessen Terrasse eine breite, weisse Marmortreppe in den angrenzenden Park führte. Er machte sich gleich ans Werk. Tagelang musste er arbeiten, um all das, was er gepflanzt hatte, zum Blühen zu bringen.

ville qu'il avait sauvée de son éternelle grisaille. Il y aimait aussi les gens. Mais il voulait satisfaire tous les désirs de sa femme car il éprouvait beaucoup d'amour pour elle.

Le jour suivant, il se rendit dans la grande ville et découvrit tous ses beaux édifices, tout son luxe et son animation, mais aussi tous ses bruits et toute sa poussière. Il trouva bientôt un palais magnifique, aux majestueuses marches de marbre blanc qui menaient de la terrasse au parc attenant. Il se mit immédiatement au travail. Il lui fallut plusieurs jours pour faire fleurir tout ce qu'il avait planté.

pequeño pueblo que él mismo había salvado de su eterna condición gris. También quería a la gente. Pero quería cumplir los deseos de su esposa, porque la amaba inmensamente.

Al día siguiente viajó a la gran ciudad, con todos sus excelentes edificios, todo su lujo y atractivos, pero también, con todo su ruido y polvo. Pronto halló un magnífico palacio, cuyas amplias escalinatas de mármol blanco conducían desde la terraza hasta el parque adyacente. Inmediatamente empezó a trabajar. Le tomó varios días hacer florecer cuanto había plantado.

53

When the park's gardeners saw the man kneeling in the flower beds, they started to laugh for in the big city gentlemen do not kneel in flower beds. But after a few days, when the park began to overflow with blossoms, the gardeners realized they had been watching a flower magician. They stopped laughing and tried to find out how the man had created all of this splendor.

The wife was happy now. She purchased the most expensive dresses and was soon attending the king's receptions. She was admired for her beauty and was invited

Als die Gärtner des Parks den Mann in den Beeten knien sahen, begannen sie ihn auszulachen, denn in der grossen Stadt kniet die Herrschaft nicht in Blumenbeeten. Doch als nach ein paar Tagen der Park von Blüten überquoll, da wussten auch die Gärtner, dass hier ein Blütenzauberer am Werk gewesen war. Sie hörten auf zu lachen und versuchten zu ergründen, wie der Mann all die Pracht zustande gebracht hatte.

Die Frau war nun zufrieden. Sie kaufte die teuersten Kleider und besuchte die Empfänge des Königs. Sie wurde ob ihrer Schönheit bewundert und überall einge-

Quand les jardiniers du parc virent l'homme agenouillé sur les parterres de fleurs, ils se mirent à rire, car dans la grande ville, les messieurs ne s'agenouillent pas sur les parterres. Mais quelques jours plus tard, quand le parc regorgea de fleurs, les jardiniers se rendirent compte qu'ils avaient à faire à un magicien des fleurs. Ils cessèrent d'en rire et essayèrent de découvrir comment cet homme avait créé une telle splendeur.

Sa femme était heureuse, maintenant. Elle achetait les robes les plus coûteuses, et assista bientôt aux réceptions du roi. On l'admirait pour sa beauté et on l'invitait partout.

Cuando los jardineros del parque lo vieron arrodillado sobre los lechos de flores, se rieron de él, pues en la gran ciudad los caballeros no se hincan sobre lechos de flores. Pero después de varios días, cuando el parque se llenó de retoños, los jardineros se percataron de que habían estado observando a un mago de las flores. Dejaron de reírse y trataron de averiguar cómo había creado tal esplendor aquel hombre.

La esposa era ahora feliz. Compró los vestidos más caros y pronto estaba asistiendo a las recepciones del rey. Ahí, era admirada por su belleza e invitada a todas partes.

everywhere. And always when she returned home, she found the most beautiful flower arrangements that her husband had created for her. This life of luxury and comfort pleased her for a long time.

One morning, however, when the woman looked into the mirror, she realized how old she was beginning to look. With a bit of make-up she could still hide her wrinkles, but she knew it would not be long before others would notice that her beauty was fading. She was determined to prevent this.

laden. Kam sie jedoch nach Hause, so fand sie die prächtigsten Blumenarrangements vor, die der Mann für sie geschaffen hatte. Dieses Leben in Luxus und Bequemlichkeit gefiel ihr lange Zeit.

Doch eines Morgens, als die Frau in den Spiegel blickte, gewahrte sie, wie alt sie geworden war. Zwar konnte sie mit Schminke die Falten übertünchen, doch würde es nicht lange dauern, bis auch andere den Verfall ihrer Schönheit wahrnehmen würden. Das wollte sie verhindern.

Lorsqu'elle rentrait à la maison, elle trouvait les compositions florales les plus étourdissantes, créées pour elle par son mari. Cette vie de luxe et de confort l'enchanta pendant longtemps.

Mais un matin qu'elle se regardait dans le miroir, la femme vit combien elle avait vieilli. Avec un peu de maquillage, elle pouvait encore dissimuler ses rides, mais elle était sûre que d'ici peu, les autres pourraient remarquer que sa beauté se fanait. Elle était décidée à l'éviter.

Y cuando regresaba a casa, encontraba los más bellos arreglos florales, creados para ella por su esposo. Esta vida de lujo y comodidad le satisfizo por mucho tiempo.

Una mañana, sin embargo, cuando la mujer miró en el espejo, se dio cuenta de lo vieja que se había hecho. Con un poco de cosméticos podía esconder sus arrugas, pero sabía que pronto los demás se darían cuenta de que su belleza estaba desapareciendo. Estaba decidida a evitar esto.

She remembered hearing about an island where time seemed to stand still and the sun shone every day. Right away she said to her husband, "I am tired of living here in the capital with its shallow people and superficial lifestyle. I am tired of the park. I am tired of your flowers. Get us a house on an island, where the sun shines every day and the sandy white shores stretch to meet the blue sea."

The man was very discouraged when he heard these words. But the next morning he set out to sea in search of an island to please her.

Ihr fiel ein, von einer Insel gehört zu haben, wo die Zeit stillzustehen schien und jeden Tag die Sonne leuchtete. Da sagte sie zu ihrem Mann: "Mich langweilt das Leben hier in der grossen Stadt mit all der seichten Gesellschaft und den oberflächlichen Unterhaltungen. Mich langweilt der Park. Mich langweilen deine Blumen. Schaff uns ein Haus auf einer Insel, wo jeden Tag die Sonne scheint und der weisse Sandstrand bis an das blaue Meer reicht."

Der Mann war über ihre Worte sehr betrübt. Doch tags darauf schon fuhr er fort, auf der Suche nach einer Insel, die ihr gefiel.

Puis elle se souvint avoir entendu parler d'une île oû le temps semblait s'être arrêté et où le soleil brillait chaque jour. C'est alors qu'elle dit à son mari: «Je suis lasse de la vie ici, avec ces gens superficiels et cette existence futile. Je suis lasse du parc. Je suis lasse de tes fleurs. Trouve-nous une maison sur une île, là où le soleil brille tous les jours, et les rivages de sable blanc s'étirent jusqu'à la mer bleue.»

L'homme fut consterné d'entendre ces paroles. Mais le matin suivant, il partit en mer à la recherche d'une île pour lui faire plaisir.

Entonces recordó haber oído hablar de una isla donde el tiempo parecía detenerse y donde el sol brillaba cada día. En ese instante, le dijo a su marido: —Yo estoy cansada de vivir aquí en la capital con su gente vacía y estilo de vida superficial. Estoy cansada del parque. Estoy cansada de tus flores. ¡Consíguenos una casa en la isla, donde el sol brilla cada día y la arenosa costa blanca se extiende hasta encontrar el mar!

El hombre se consternó al oír estas palabras, pero a la siguiente mañana, salió a navegar en busca de una isla para complacerla.

While the boat was gliding over the waves, he thought of all the gardens he had created to bring joy to his wife's eyes. Now he realized how little it had meant to her and knowing this caused him great disappointment. The longer he sailed over the waves, the more sorrowful he became, until he was filled with grief.

At last he landed on an island with a beautiful villa built on its slopes. The garden descended in graceful terraces down to the sandy white shore and the blue ocean beyond.

Während das Schiff über die Wellen glitt, erinnerte er sich all der Gärten, die er geschaffen hatte, um seiner Frau Freude zu bereiten. Doch nun erkannte er, wie wenig es ihr bedeutet hatte. Er war darüber sehr enttäuscht. Je länger das Schiff ihn über die Wellen trug, desto unglücklicher wurde er, bis er schliesslich ganz von Trauer erfüllt war.

Endlich gelangte er zu einer Insel, an deren Abhang eine wunderschöne Villa stand. Der Garten fiel in Terrassen hinab zum weissen Sandstrand am blauen Meer.

Tandis que le bateau glissait sur les ondes, il pensait à tous les jardins qu'il avait créés pour mettre de la joie dans les yeux de sa femme. Seulement, il se rendait maintenant compte du peu que cela avait representé pour elle. Cette prise de conscience le désappointa profondément. Plus il naviguait sur les ondes, plus il était triste, jusqu'à être débordé de chagrin.

Il aborda enfin une île. Une jolie villa se trouvait sur un coteau. Le jardin descendait en belles terrasses jusqu'au rivage de sable blanc et à la mer bleue.

Mientras el barco se deslizaba sobre las olas, recordaba todos los jardines que había creado para darle alegría a su esposa. Sin embargo, ahora se percataba de cuán poco le habían importado. El saber esto le provocaba una gran desilusión. Mientras más navegaba sobre las olas, más afligido se sentía, hasta que se llenó de dolor.

Finalmente desembarcó en una isla. Una hermosa villa estaba situada sobre su cuesta. El jardín descendía en graciosas terrazas hacia la arenosa costa blanca y el azul océano un poco más allá.

The man immediately knelt down to plant his flowers, but was filled with such sadness that it extended down to his fingertips, and his thoughts remained gloomy. When he finally finished planting, he returned home to get his wife.

They had to sail for several days before reaching the island. At last they spotted the shore and the villa gleaming a radiant white. But as they entered the garden leading down to the white sandy beach, the wife saw it was filled with vines of black roses.

Schnell kniete der Mann nieder, um seine Blumen zu setzen, doch Traurigkeit erfüllte ihn bis in die Fingerspitzen und seine Gedanken blieben düster. Als er endlich mit dem Pflanzen fertig war, fuhr er zurück, um seine Frau zu holen.

Sie mussten etliche Tage segeln, um zu der Insel zu gelangen. Endlich enblickten sie das Ufer, und die Villa leuchtete ihnen strahlend weiss entgegen. Doch als sie den Garten betraten, der hinunterführte zum weissen Strand, da erblickte die Frau nur schwarze Rosenranken.

L'homme s'agenouilla tout de suite pour planter ses fleurs, mais il était plein de tristesse, jusqu'au bout des ongles, et ses pensées demeuraient sombres. Lorsqu'il eut enfin fini de tout planter, il retourna chercher sa femme.

Ils leur fallut naviguer plusieurs jours avant d'atteindre l'île. Finalement, ils aperçurent la plage et la villa rayonnante de blancheur. Mais lorsqu'ils pénétrèrent dans le jardin qui menait à la plage de sable blanc, la femme vit qu'il était rempli de rosiers noirs.

Rápidamente, el hombre se arrodilló para plantar sus flores, pero el pesar le llenaba hasta la yema de los dedos y sus pensamientos seguían llenos de tristeza. Cuando finalmente terminó de plantar, regresó a casa para traer a su esposa.

Tuvieron que navegar por varios días antes de llegar a la isla. Finalmente avistaron la costa y la villa que destellaba un blanco radiante. Pero al entrar al jardín que conducía a la arenosa playa blanca, la esposa notó que estaba llena de enredaderas de rosas negras.

"Why didn't you plant bright flowers?" she asked in bewilderment. It was as though she had noticed his work for the very first time.

"Bring me some colorful flowers!" she snapped. But he shrugged his shoulders helplessly and looked at her with overwhelming sadness. He knew she had destroyed all the joy within him.

The wife did not understand his look of sorrow. Instead she went on, "If you can't do it yourself, get me a gardener, and you can go back to your hick village!"

"Warum hast du keine bunten Blumen gepflanzt?" fragte sie erschrocken. Es schien, als hätte sie zum ersten Mal im Leben seine Arbeit wahrgenommen.

"Schaff bunte Blumen her", herrschte sie den Mann an. Der zuckte nur hilflos mit den Schultern und blickte sie unendlich traurig an. Er wusste, dass sie in ihm jede innere Freude erstickt hatte.

Die Frau verstand den Ausdruck seiner Trauer nicht. Statt dessen fuhr sie unbarmherzig fort: "Wenn du es selbst nicht zustandebringst, dann hol einen Gärtner, und du geh zurück in dein Kuhdorf!"

«Pourquoi n'as-tu pas planté des fleurs de couleurs gaies?» demanda-t-elle, ahurie. On aurait dit qu'elle remarquait son travail pour la première fois de sa vie.

«Mets des fleurs de couleurs vives!» ordonna-t-elle d'un ton sec. Mais il haussa les épaules d'impuissance et la regarda avec une immense tristesse. Il savait qu'elle avait détruit toute joie en lui.

Sa femme ne comprit pas son regard affligé. Elle poursuivit: «Si tu n'es pas capable de le faire toi-même, fais venir un jardinier, et toi, tu peux retourner dans ton village de grossiers paysans!»

—¿Porqué no plantaste flores brillantes? —preguntó confundida—. Parecía ser la primera vez que notaba su trabajo. —¡Tráeme algunas flores pintorescas! —dijo ásperamente—. Pero él tan sólo se encogió de hombros impotentemente y la miró con abrumadora tristeza. Sabía que ella había destruido toda la alegría dentro de él.

La esposa no entendió su mirada de aflicción. En vez de ello continuó:

—Si no lo puedes hacer por ti mismo, consígueme un jardinero, ¡y tú puedes regresarte a tu querido pueblo de campesinos!

At that, the husband turned without a word and strode down to the beach. He climbed into the boat and headed out to sea.

The woman remained on the island, where the strange black roses grew from every side. No gardener was ever able to control their growth and soon the heavy vines formed an impenetrable thicket, holding the wife prisoner on the island.

The man returned to the village of his youth. He moved into the cottage at the edge of the village, and

Da kehrte der Mann ihr wortlos den Rücken und eilte hinunter an den Strand. Er bestieg das Schiff und segelte davon.

Die Frau aber blieb zurück auf der Insel, wo die wundersamen, schwarzen Rosen von allen Seiten wucherten. Kein Gärtner vermochte den Wuchs einzudämmen, und bald formten die schweren Ranken eine undurchdringliche Hecke, welche die Frau auf der Insel gefangen hielt.

Der Mann aber fuhr zurück in das Dorf seiner Jugend. Er bezog das kleine Haus am Rand des Dorfes, und kaum

Alors le mari tourna les talons sans rien dire et s'en alla vers la plage à grands pas. Il s'embarqua et repartit en mer.

La femme resta sur l'île, où les étranges roses noires poussaient de tous côtés. Aucun jardinier ne parvint à empêcher leur prolifération, si bien que les épais rosiers formèrent rapidement une haie impénétrable, qui gardait la femme prisonnière sur l'île.

L'homme retourna au village de sa jeunesse. Il s'installa dans la petite maison à la lisière du village et dès qu'il

Ante ello, el esposo se volteó sin pronunciar una palabra y bajó a trancos hacia la playa. Subió al bote y se dirigió al mar.

La mujer se quedó en la isla, donde las extrañas flores negras crecían por todos lados. Ningún jardinero jamás fue capaz de controlar su crecimiento y pronto la pesada enredadera formó una maleza impenetrable, manteniendo a la esposa prisionera en la isla.

El hombre retornó al pueblo de su juventud. Se mudó a la cabaña situada a las orillas del pueblo, y casi tan

almost as soon as he knelt down in his garden, the beautiful flowers he had planted there years earlier began to blossom again.

kniete er in seinem Garten nieder, so begannen die wundervollen Blumen, die er Jahre zuvor gepflanzt hatte, von neuem wieder zu spriessen.

s'agenouilla dans son jardin, les belles fleurs qu'il avait plantées là des années auparavant se remirent à pousser.

pronto como se arrodilló en su jardín, las hermosas flores que había plantado ahí años atrás comenzaron a retoñar de nuevo.

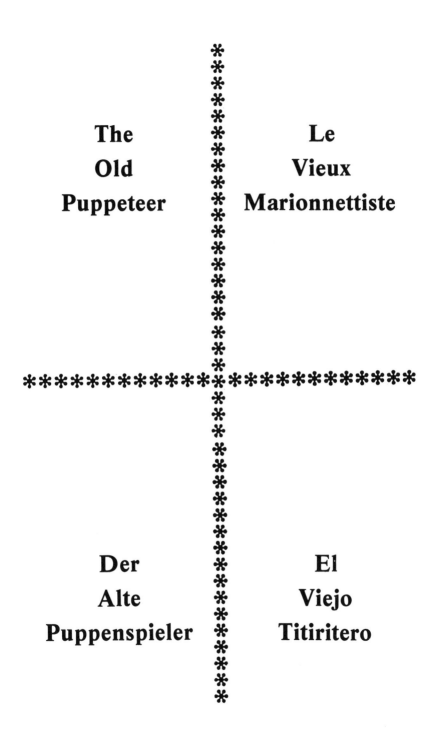

The
Old
Puppeteer

Le
Vieux
Marionnettiste

Der
Alte
Puppenspieler

El
Viejo
Titiritero

Every year, just before Christmas, the old puppeteer came to the little town. He would put up his stage in the middle of the marketplace. The youngsters could sit comfortably on the steps of the city hall and watch his performance while the grown-ups eagerly hurried from one shop to the next, from the shoemaker to the flower shop or yarn store, or even to the little coffee house for a cup of steaming chocolate.

The children watched wide-eyed as the old magician in the puppet show abducted the young princess. Then, when the handsome prince suddenly emerged from the

✳✳✳✳✳✳✳✳✳✳✳✳✳✳✳✳✳✳✳✳✳✳

Alljährlich zur Vorweihnachtszeit kam der alte Puppenspieler in die kleine Stadt. Er errichtete seine Bühne mitten auf dem Marktplatz. Die Kinder konnten bequem auf den Stufen, die zum Rathaus hinaufführten, sitzen und der Vorstellung folgen, während die Erwachsenen eifrig von einem Geschäft zum anderen liefen, vom Schuster zum Blumenladen, dann ins Strickwarengeschäft oder gar in das kleine Kaffeehaus, um eine Tasse Schokolade zu trinken.

Die Kinder sahen mit grossen Augen geängstigt zu, wie der alte Zauberer die zarte Prinzessin entführte. Kam dann der junge Prinz aus dem Dickicht der Baumkulisse

Chaque année, juste avant Noël, le vieux marionnettiste se rendait dans la petite ville. Il montait son théâtre au milieu de la place du Marché. Les enfants pouvaient s'installer sur les marches de l'Hôtel de Ville et regarder le spectacle, tandis que les aînés couraient d'une boutique à l'autre, du cordonnier au fleuriste, ou à la mercerie, ou encore au petit salon de thé pour y prendre une tasse de chocolat chaud.

Les enfants regardaient, les yeux écarquillés, l'enlèvement de la jeune princesse par le vieux magicien de la troupe. Ensuite, lorsque le séduisant prince apparaissait

✻✻✻✻✻✻✻✻✻✻✻✻✻✻✻✻✻✻✻✻✻✻✻

Cada año, justo antes de Navidad, el viejo titiritero llegaba a la pequeña ciudad. Alzaba su teatro en medio de la plaza del Mercado. Los jóvenes podían sentarse confortablemente en las escalinatas del ayuntamiento y ver su espectáculo, mientras los mayores se apresuraban de una tienda a otra, del zapatero a la tienda de flores, a la mercería, o al pequeño café para tomar una taza de chocolate humeante.

Los niños, enarcando las cejas ante el espectáculo de títeres, miraban como el viejo mago raptaba a la joven princesa. Luego, cuando el joven príncipe emergía de pronto

backdrop of trees and asked where the princess was being held captive, the children would all yell out, "At the magician's—at the magician's!"

Tears of relief streamed down their young cheeks when the villain was finally defeated, yielded up his lovely victim and disappeared into the bottomless pit. Then the gallant prince would carry the damsel home to his castle.

The jubilation of the little spectators meant much more to the puppeteer than the few coins passers-by had thrown into the hat placed in front of the stage. With deep

✽✽✽✽✽✽✽✽✽✽✽✽✽✽✽✽✽✽✽✽✽✽

hervor und fragte, wo die Prinzessin gefangen gehalten werde, dann schrien die Kinder aus vollem Hals: "Beim Zauberer, beim Zauberer!"

Tränen der Erleichterung strömten über die runden Backen, sobald der Bösewicht, endlich besiegt, sein junges Opfer freigab und vernichtet ins Bodenlose versank, während der Prinz das Mädchen auf sein Schloss heimführte.

Der Jubel der kleinen Zuschauer bedeutete dem Puppenspieler weit mehr, als die wenigen Münzen, die man in den vor der Bühne aufgestellten Hut geworfen hatte. Mit

devant le rideau d'arbres et demandait où la princesse était captive, les enfants se mettaient tous à crier: «Chez le magicien, chez le magicien!»

Des larmes de soulagement coulaient sur leurs joues d'enfants lorsque le vilain, enfin vaincu, relâchait sa jolie victime et disparaissait dans un trou sans fond. Alors, le vaillant prince reconduisait la demoiselle à son château.

Aux yeux du marionnettiste la joie des petits spectateurs avait plus de valeur que les quelques pièces jetées par les passants dans le chapeau placé devant l'estrade.

✳✳✳✳✳✳✳✳✳✳✳✳✳✳✳✳✳✳✳✳✳✳✳

de la cortina de árboles y preguntaba dónde la guardaban prisionera, los niños gritaban todos: —¡En casa del mago, en casa del mago!

Lágrimas de alivio corrían por sus mejillas de niños cuando el villano, vencido finalmente, entregaba a su hermosa víctima y desaparecía en el hoyo sin fondo. Entonces, el caballeroso príncipe llevaba a la doncella a su castillo.

Le importaba más al titiritero el júbilo de los pequeños espectadores que las cuantas monedas echadas por los transeúntes en el sombrero colocado enfrente del escenario.

satisfaction, he listened to the cheers and applause at the end of the performance. Then he carefully laid the puppets on the table, smoothed the long strings with which he directed their movements and arranged their garments.

"Today you gave a really splendid performance," he told them, smiling, "an outstanding effort." "Well done, my friend," he added as he cleaned the prince's green velvet suit with a clothes brush. Then he merely blew on the cap and its arched plume so as not to damage the delicate embroidery.

✳✳✳✳✳✳✳✳✳✳✳✳✳✳✳✳✳✳✳✳✳✳✳✳

tiefer Befriedigung lauschte er dem Applaus am Ende der Vorstellung, während er die Puppen sorgfältig auf den Tisch legte, die langen Fäden, mit denen er die Glieder dirigierte, glatt strich und ihre Kleider in Ordnung brachte.

"Heute habt ihr eine wirklich gute Vorstellung gegeben", meinte er lobend, "eine hervorragende Leistung. Gut gemacht, mein Freund", fügte er hinzu, als er mit einer Kleiderbürste den grünen Samtanzug des Prinzen säuberte. Die Mütze mit der geschwungenen Feder blies er allerdings nur ab, um die empfindliche Verbrämung nicht zu beschädigen.

C'est avec une profonde satisfaction qu'il entendait les applaudissements et les rappels à la fin de la représentation. Puis il posait soigneusement les marionnettes sur la table, lissait les longs fils qui lui servaient à diriger leurs mouvements et arrangeait leurs habits.

«Aujourd'hui, vous avez donné une représentation tout à fait splendide» leur dit-il en souriant, «une prestation remarquable! Bien joué, mon ami» ajouta-t-il tout en brossant le pourpoint de velours vert du prince. Puis il souffla légèrement sur le chapeau et sa plume recourbée pour ne pas abîmer les délicates broderies.

✳✳✳✳✳✳✳✳✳✳✳✳✳✳✳✳✳✳✳✳✳✳✳✳

Con profunda satisfacción oía los bravos y los aplausos al final de la función. Luego, colocaba con precaución los títeres sobre la mesa, alisaba los largos hilos con los cuales dirigía sus movimientos, y arreglaba sus prendas.

—Hoy, habéis dado una representación verdaderamente espléndida —les dijo sonriente—, un esfuerzo excepcional. Bien trabajado, amigo mio —añadió, cepillando el traje de terciopelo verde del príncipe. Después, sopló ligeramente en el sombrero y en su pluma curvada para no estropear el bordado delicado.

Even lying there on the table, the magician puppet in his red cape with the black silk suit visible beneath, appeared to inspire fear. "You mustn't overact," the puppeteer told him. "The little ones are very afraid of you. They might run away, and we wouldn't want that."

The magician didn't answer. Instead, looking somewhat annoyed, he turned away as the puppeteer placed him carefully into a case lined with blue velvet that he had specially made for his puppets. There, they lay together peacefully, side by side, all except for one—the princess.

✶✶✶✶✶✶✶✶✶✶✶✶✶✶✶✶✶✶✶✶✶

Der Zauberer in seinem roten Umhang, unter welchem ein schwarzer Seidenanzug sichtbar wurde, sah auch auf dem Tisch furchterregend aus. "Du musst deine Rolle nicht übertreiben", meinte der Puppenspieler zu ihm. "Die Kinder fürchten sich schrecklich vor dir. Sie könnten uns einmal davonlaufen, und das wollen wir doch nicht."

Der Zauberer gab darauf gar keine Antwort. Vielmehr wandte er verärgert den Kopf ab, als der Puppenspieler die Figur vorsichtig in einen mit blauem Samt ausgeschlagenen Koffer legte, den er eigens für seine Puppen hatte anfertigen lassen. Da lagen sie nun alle friedlich nebeneinander; alle bis auf eine - die Prinzessin.

Même étendu là, sur la table, le magicien articulé vêtu de sa cape rouge sous laquelle on voyait son costume de soie noire, suscitait la crainte. «Il ne faut pas trop en remettre», lui dit le marionnettiste. «Les petits ont très peur de toi. Si tu exagères, ils pourraient s'en aller, ce que nous ne voulons pas.»

Le magicien ne répondit pas. Au contraire, apparemment un peu irrité, il tourna le dos lorsque le marionnettiste le plaça avec soin dans la boîte doublée de velours bleu qu'il avait fait faire spécialement pour ses marionnettes. C'est là qu'elles restaient toutes, paisiblement, l'une à côté de l'autre, sauf une: la princesse.

✶✶✶✶✶✶✶✶✶✶✶✶✶✶✶✶✶✶✶✶✶✶✶✶

Aun tendido allí sobre la mesa, el títere-mago, vestido con su capa roja que dejaba ver su traje de seda negra, parecía impresionar.

—No debes exagerar —le dijo el titiritero—. Los chiquillos te tienen mucho miedo. Si actúas demasiado, pueden huír y no es lo que deseamos.

El mago no contestó. En cambio, pareciendo algo irritado, volvió la espalda cuando el titiritero lo colocó con cuidado en una caja doblada con terciopelo azul que había encargado especialmente para sus títeres. Allí estaban todos tranquilos, uno junto al otro, excepto la princesa.

Gently, the puppeteer's fingers touched the fine features of her porcelain face. Then he smoothed the silken hair and adjusted the delicate lace collar. The pink silk dress rustled as the old man picked her up.

"You are growing more beautiful every day," he whispered, letting her do a few dance steps on the table. The princess bowed and, with one hand, lifted her silk skirt a bit until her white satin shoes came into view.

"Enough for today," admonished the puppeteer and started to put her into the case, but she looked at him pleadingly.

✽✽✽✽✽✽✽✽✽✽✽✽✽✽✽✽✽✽✽✽✽

Behutsam fuhren die Finger des Puppenspielers über ihr feines Porzellangesicht. Er streichelte das seidige Haar und zupfte die Spitzenkrause zurecht. Das rosa Seidenkleid raschelte, als der alte Mann sie vom Tisch hochhob.

"Du wirst von Tag zu Tag schöner", flüsterte er ihr zu und liess sie ein paar Tanzschritte machen. Die Prinzessin verbeugte sich und hob mit der Hand ein wenig den Seidenrock, sodass ihre weissen Satinschuhe sichtbar wurden.

"Genug für heute", ermahnte der Puppenspieler und machte Anstalten, auch sie in den Koffer zu legen. Sie aber sah ihn flehend an.

Doucement, le marionnettiste fit courir ses doigts sur les traits délicats du visage de porcelaine. Puis il lissa les cheveux soyeux et ajusta le col de fine dentelle. La robe de soie rose bruissa lorsque le vieil homme la prit entre ses mains.

«Tu deviens plus belle de jour en jour» murmura-t-il en la laissant faire quelques pas de danse sur la table. La princesse fit la révérence et, d'une main, releva légèrement sa jupe de soie, laissant voir ses souliers de satin blanc.

«Cela suffit pour aujourd'hui», gronda le marionnettiste, et il voulut la remettre dans la boîte, mais elle leva vers lui un regard suppliant.

✳✳✳✳✳✳✳✳✳✳✳✳✳✳✳✳✳✳✳✳✳✳

Suavemente, los dedos del titiritero tocaron los finos rasgos de su cara de porcelana. Luego alisaron los cabellos sedosos y ajustaron el cuello de encaje delicado. El vestido de seda rosada crujió cuando el viejo hombre la tomó en sus manos.

—Te vuelves cada día más bella —susurró, dejándola hacer unos pasos de baile sobre la mesa. La princesa hizo una reverencia, y con una mano, levantó un poco su falda de seda, dejando ver sus zapatos de satén blanco.

—Basta por hoy —la amonestó el titiritero, e iba a ponerla en la caja, pero ella lo miró, suplicante.

"Let me dance a little more," she begged. "I don't like being locked up in the case. It is so dark and boring there. Besides, nobody can see how beautiful I am," she added coquettishly.

With that, she pirouetted in a circle until her skirt surrounded her like a bell. "Why don't you let us have some fun once in a while?" she reproached him. "We always have to be ready for you. There is either a rehearsal or a performance, or you clean and straighten our clothes, but the moment you are through you put us back into the case and close the lid. Do you think that is a pleasant life?"

✳✳✳✳✳✳✳✳✳✳✳✳✳✳✳✳✳✳✳✳

"Lass mich noch ein bisschen hier draussen tanzen", bat sie ihn. "Ich mag nicht immer eingesperrt werden. Es ist so langweilig und düster in dem Kasten. Ausserdem sieht dann niemand, wie schön ich bin", fügte sie kokett hinzu.

Dabei drehte sie sich im Kreis, so dass ihr Rock sie wie eine Glocke umgab. "Warum gönnst du uns nicht auch einmal etwas Spass?" fuhr sie vorwurfsvoll fort. "Immer müssen wir für dich bereit sein. Entweder wir proben, oder wir haben Vorstellung, oder du zupfst an uns herum. Doch kaum bist du fertig, so steckst du uns in den Koffer und klappst den Deckel zu. Glaubst du, dass so ein Leben uns angenehm ist?"

«Laisse-moi danser encore un peu», le pria-t-elle. «Je n'aime pas être enfermée dans cette boîte. C'est si sombre et si ennuyeux. Et en plus, personne ne peut voir combien je suis belle» ajouta-t-elle avec coquetterie.

Alors, elle fit un cercle de piróuettes, jusqu'à ce que sa jupe formât une cloche autour d'elle. «Pourquoi ne nous laisses-tu pas nous amuser de temps en temps?» lui reprocha-t-elle. «Il faut que nous soyons toujours à ta disposition, soit pour une répétition, soit pour une représentation, ou bien tu nettoies et tu arranges nos habits. Mais dès que tu as fini, tu nous remets dans la boîte et tu fermes le couvercle. Crois-tu que c'est une vie agréable?»

✳✳✳✳✳✳✳✳✳✳✳✳✳✳✳✳✳✳✳✳✳

—Déjame que baile un poco más —le rogó—. No me gusta estar encerrada en esa caja. Es tan oscuro y tan aburrido allí. Además, nadie puede ver lo hermosa que soy —añadió con coquetería.

Diciendo esto, hizo piruetas en un círculo hasta que su falda la rodeó como una campana. —¿Por qué no nos dejas divertirnos de vez en cuando? —le reprochó ella—. Siempre tenemos que estar a tu disposición. Hay ya una repetición, ya una función, o limpias y arreglas nuestra ropa, pero apenas has terminado, nos pones otra vez en la caja y cierras la tapa. ¿Crees que la nuestra es una vida agradable?

These words hurt the puppeteer very deeply because he cared for his puppets as a father would, ordering splendid costumes for them to wear, sheltering and protecting them from damage.

He shook his head and, looking at the princess, he said quietly, "You have no right to talk like that. From morning until night, my thoughts are only about all of you. I create the best plays for you, and you are the most popular puppets in the entire country. I don't do it for myself. After all, nobody sees me, nobody knows me. I merely stand behind the stage," he went on, "but you have the success— and you deserve it. I only want the best for you."

✳✳✳✳✳✳✳✳✳✳✳✳✳✳✳✳✳✳✳✳✳✳✳✳

Diese Worte kränkten den Puppenspieler sehr, denn er pflegte seine Puppen wie ein Vater, liess ihnen die schönsten Kostüme schneidern, umsorgte sie und behütete sie vor jedem Schaden.

Kopfschüttelnd betrachtete er die Prinzessin und meinte dann ruhig: "Du hast kein Recht, so mit mir zu sprechen. Von früh bis spät kreisen meine Gedanken nur um euch. Ich erfinde für euch die besten Rollen, die euch zur beliebtesten Marionettengruppe im ganzen Land gemacht haben. Ich tue es nicht für mich. Mich sieht und kennt man nicht einmal. Ich stehe hinter der Bühne. Ihr habt den Erfolg, und er gebührt euch auch. Ich will für euch das Beste."

Ces paroles blessèrent profondément le marionnet-tiste car il aimait ses marionnettes comme un père; il leur faisait porter de splendides costumes et les mettait soigneusement à l'abri du moindre dommage.

Il secoua la tête et, regardant la princesse, dit doucement: «Tu n'as pas le droit de parler ainsi. Du matin au soir, je n'ai de pensée que pour vous. Je crée les meilleures pièces pour vous, et vous êtes les marionnettes les plus célèbres de tout le pays. Je ne le fais pas pour moi. Après tout, personne ne me voit, personne ne me connaît. Je me tiens seulement derrière la scène, poursuivit-il, mais c'est vous qui connaissez le succès, et vous le méritez. Je ne veux que ce qu'il y a de mieux pour vous.»

✳✳✳✳✳✳✳✳✳✳✳✳✳✳✳✳✳✳✳✳✳✳

Estas palabras le hirieron profundamente al titiritero porque quería a sus títeres como un padre, encargando trajes espléndidos para que los lucieran, y protegiéndolos de todo daño.

Meneó la cabeza y mirando a la princesa dijo apacible: —No tienes derecho de hablar así. De la mañana a la noche, no tengo pensamientos sino para vosotros. Elaboro las mejores obras para vosotros, y sois las marionetas más famosas de todo el país. No lo hago por mí. Después de todo, no me ve nadie, no me conoce nadie. Sólo me quedo detrás del escenario, —prosiguió—, pero vosotros tenéis el éxito y os lo merecéis. No quiero sino lo mejor para vosotros.

With these words, he lowered the princess into the case and quickly closed the lid. He did not want to hear any more back talk. There the princess lay on her blue velvet bed, feeling alone and unhappy. What good was it being sheltered? What good were these beautiful clothes? She longed to be with people, friends, companions. Tears rolled down her cheeks, and her sobs soon woke the other puppets.

"The princess is crying," they whispered to one another. She must be very sad, thought the country bumpkin, who always fell on his face when he stepped onto the puppet stage.

�✳✳✳✳✳✳✳✳✳✳✳✳✳✳✳✳✳✳✳✳✳✳

Mit diesen Worten legte er die Prinzessin in den Koffer und machte schnell den Deckel zu, denn er wollte keine Widerrede hören. Da lag sie nun in ihrem blauen Samtbett, allein und unglücklich. Was half ihr das Behütetsein, wozu dienten die schönen Kleider? Sie sehnte sich nach Menschen, nach Freunden, Gefährten. Tränen rollten über ihre Wangen, und ihr Schluchzen weckte die anderen Puppen.

"Die Prinzessin weint", flüsterten sie einander zu. Sie muss sehr unglücklich sein, überlegte der Bauerntölpel, der immer auf die Nase fiel, sobald er die Bühne betrat.

Ce disant, il posa la princesse dans la boîte et referma vite le couvercle. Il ne voulait plus entendre de récriminations. La princesse reposait là, sur son lit de velours bleu, se sentant seule et triste. A quoi bon être protégée, à quoi bon porter ces beaux habits? Elle avait envie d'être avec des gens, des amis, des compagnons. Les larmes roulaient sur ses joues et bientôt ses sanglots réveillèrent les autres marionnettes.

«La princesse pleure» chuchotaient-elles entre elles. Elle doit être bien malheureuse, pensa l'innocent du village, qui tombait toujours sur la face lorsqu'il montait sur scène.

✻✻✻✻✻✻✻✻✻✻✻✻✻✻✻✻✻✻✻✻✻

Con estas palabras, colocó la princesa en la caja y cerró la tapa rápidamente. Ya no quería oír más recriminaciones. Ahí estaba la princesa sobre su lecho de terciopelo azul, sintiéndose sola y desdichada. ¿Qué había de bueno en ser protegida? ¿Qué había de bueno en lucir esos bellos vestidos? Deseaba estar con la gente, con amigos, con compañeros. Le corrieron lágrimas por las mejillas y sus sollozos despertaron a los otros títeres.

—La princesa está llorando —se susurraban el uno al otro—. «Debe de estar muy triste» pensó el tonto del pueblo que siempre se caía de cabeza al subir al escenario.

"No wonder, after her quarrel with the master," exclaimed the old lady puppet, who always had to play the witch. She was very jealous of all the applause the young princess received and didn't care for her a bit. "What does she have to be unhappy about?" the old woman snapped. "The princess has everything she needs, and she is his favorite." "If you ask me," she went on, "the master should treat her much more sternly. He should make her play the witch once in a while and do some hard work rather than pampering her."

✳✳✳✳✳✳✳✳✳✳✳✳✳✳✳✳✳✳✳✳✳✳

"Kein Wunder, nach dem Streit mit dem Meister", ereiferte sich die alte Frau, die immer die Hexe spielen musste. Sie war auf die Prinzessin sehr eifersüchtig und konnte das junge Ding nicht leiden. "Was will diese Person eigentlich?" fragte sie ungeduldig. "Sie hat doch alles, was sie braucht und wird noch dazu bevorzugt. Meiner Meinung nach", fuhr sie fort, "sollte der Meister sie viel strenger behandeln. Er sollte sie einmal die Hexe spielen lassen und ihr härtere Arbeit zuweisen, statt sie immer zu verwöhnen."

«Ce n'est pas étonnant, après sa querelle avec le maître» s'écria la vieille dame-marionnette dont le rôle était toujours de jouer la sorcière. Elle était très jalouse de tous les applaudissements que la jeune princesse recevait et n'avait aucune affection pour elle. «Quelle raison a-t-elle d'être malheureuse?» demanda sèchement la vieille femme. «La princesse a tout ce qu'il lui faut, et elle est sa favorite. Si vous voulez mon avis, poursuivit-elle, le maître devrait la traiter bien plus sévèrement. Il devrait lui faire jouer le rôle de la sorcière de temps en temps, et la faire travailler dur au lieu de la dorloter.»

✳✳✳✳✳✳✳✳✳✳✳✳✳✳✳✳✳✳✳✳✳✳✳

—Esto no me sorprende, después de su riña con el viejo titiritero —exclamó la vieja señora-marioneta que siempre tenía que hacer el papel de la bruja. Era muy envidiosa de todos los aplausos que recibía la joven princesa y no le tenía ningún afecto.

—¿Por qué va a ser infeliz? —preguntó la vieja mujer.

—La princesa tiene todo lo que necesita y és su favorita. Si queréis mi opinión, —prosiguió—, el amo debería ser mucho más severo con ella. Debería darle el papel de la bruja de vez en cuando, y proporcionarle algún trabajo duro, en lugar de mimarla.

The prince had a different view. He turned to his neighbor, the magician, and said pointedly, "We are young only once. When will we enjoy life if not now? All of us ought to speak out so that the master will grant us more freedom."

"Such nonsense," mumbled the magician, who was not fond of talking. "You young people have no idea of life. Freedom—wonderful, but what are you going to live on? You should be glad someone cares for you and protects you from hardships. Freedom—such nonsense. . ." Then he turned away and closed his eyes.

✳✳✳✳✳✳✳✳✳✳✳✳✳✳✳✳✳✳✳✳✳✳✳

Doch der Prinz war anderer Ansicht. Aufgebracht wandte er sich an seinen Nachbarn, den Zauberer: "Wir sind nur einmal jung", meinte er. "Wann denn sollen wir unser Leben geniessen, wenn nicht jetzt? Wir sollten alle gemeinsam protestieren, damit der Meister uns mehr Freiheit gewährt."

"So ein Unsinn", brummte der Zauberer, der eigentlich nur ungern redete. "Ihr Jungen habt keine Ahnung vom Leben. Freiheit - sehr schön, doch wovon wollt ihr leben? Seid lieber froh, dass jemand sich um euch kümmert und alle Sorgen von euch fernhält. Freiheit - so ein Unsinn", murmelte er noch einmal. Dann drehte er sich um und schloss die Augen.

Le prince était d'un autre avis. Il se tourna vers son voisin, le magicien, et lui dit tout net: «On n'est jeune qu'une fois. Quand profiterons-nous de la vie, si ce n'est maintenant? Nous devrions tous réclamer, afin que le maître nous accorde davantage de liberté.

«Quelle sottise!» grommela le magicien qui n'aimait pas beaucoup parler. «Vous les jeunes, n'avez aucune idée de ce qu'est la vie. La liberté! Magnifique! Mais de quoi allez-vous vivre? Vous devriez être heureux que quelqu'un s'occupe des vous et vous protège des épreuves. Liberté, quelle sottise...» Puis il tourna le dos et ferma les yeux.

✳✳✳✳✳✳✳✳✳✳✳✳✳✳✳✳✳✳✳✳✳✳✳

El príncipe tenía otra opinión. Se volvió hacia su vecino el mago, y dijo rotundamente: —Somos jóvenes sólo una vez. ¿Cuándo vamos a aprovechar de la vida si no lo hacemos ahora? Todos debemos clamarlo para que el amo nos otorgue más libertad.

—¡Qué tonterías! —refunfuñó el mago, al que no le gustaba hablar—. Vosotros, los jovenes, no tenéis ni idea de la vida. ¡Libertad, magnífico! Pero, ¿de qué vais a vivir? Deberíais estar contentos de que alguien os cuida y os protege de las dificultades. Libertad, ¡qué tontería! Luego se volvió de espaldas y cerró los ojos.

At last, the sobs of the princess let up, and peace and quiet settled over the puppet case again. But while the others slept, the princess pondered how she could break free and escape her confinement. And in fact, she had plenty of time to think.

It was nearly two days before the master took out his puppets again. This time, the princess knew they were in a larger town. The blare of automobile horns and the rattle of streetcars filled the air as the master removed one puppet after another from the case and placed them on a table top, ready for action.

✳✳✳✳✳✳✳✳✳✳✳✳✳✳✳✳✳✳✳✳✳

Auch das Schluchzen der Prinzessin verebbte langsam, und Ruhe legte sich über den Puppenkoffer. Während jedoch die anderen Puppen schliefen, grübelte die Prinzessin darüber, wie sie ihrer Gefangenschaft entrinnen könne. Dazu hatte sie reichlich Zeit.

Es dauerte fast zwei Tage, bevor der Meister seine Puppen wieder hervorholte. Die Prinzessin erkannte sofort, dass sie sich in einer grösseren Stadt befanden. Der Lärm hupender Autos und ratternder Strassenbahnen drang zu ihnen, sobald der Meister eine Figur nach der anderen aus dem Koffer nahm und sie spielbereit auf den Tisch legte.

Finalement, les pleurs de la princesse cessèrent, et le calme régna de nouveau dans la boîte des marionnettes. Mais tandis que les autres dormaient, la princesse se demandait comment elle pourrait se rendre libre et s'enfuir de sa prison. Et elle eut tout le temps d'y réfléchir.

Presque deux jours s'écoulèrent avant que le maître sortît de nouveau ses marionnettes. Cette fois, la princesse se rendit compte qu'ils se trouvaient dans une ville plus importante. Le retentissement des avertisseurs et le ferraillement des tramways emplissaient l'air tandis que le maître retirait l'une après l'autre les marionnettes de la boîte et les plaçait sur une table, prêtes à l'action.

✳✳✳✳✳✳✳✳✳✳✳✳✳✳✳✳✳✳✳✳✳

Finalmente, los sollozos de la princesa cesaron, y la paz y la tranquilidad volvieron a instalarse sobre la caja de los títeres. Pero mientras los otros dormían, la princesa se preguntaba como podría ser libre y huír de su prisión. Tuvo mucho tiempo para pensar.

Pasaron casi dos días antes de que el amo sacara de nuevo sus marionetas. Esta vez, la princesa se dió cuenta de que estaban en una ciudad más grande. El resonar de los claxones y el traqueteo de los tranvías llenaban el aire mientras el amo sacaba los títeres uno tras otro de la caja y los disponía sobre la mesa, preparándolos para actuar.

When the curtain finally went up, the princess was at last able to gaze out at the colorful world of which she had been deprived for so long. With her eyes, she devoured the beauty of the little park that lay before them, the playground beyond, the snack shop, the stone fountain and the snow-covered flower beds.

Above the heads of the young spectators, she spotted a young waiter standing in the doorway of the little cafe, smoking his cigarette. The princess looked at the young man in silent admiration and her heart began to beat with

✳✳✳✳✳✳✳✳✳✳✳✳✳✳✳✳✳✳✳✳✳✳✳✳

Als der Vorhang sich endlich öffnete, konnte die Prinzessin einen Blick auf die bunte Welt werfen, die ihr so lange vorenthalten worden war. Sie verschlang mit den Augen den hübschen Park, der vor ihr lag, den Kinderspielplatz, die Imbiss-Stube, den Springbrunnen und die schneebedeckten Blumenbeete.

Über die Köpfe der kleinen Zuschauer hinweg erblickte sie einen Kellner, der rauchend vor der Tür des bescheidenen Esslokales stand. Gebannt starrte die Prinzessin auf den jungen Burschen, und ihr Herz begann vor Aufregung

Quand le rideau se leva enfin, la princesse put finalement contempler le monde aux vives couleurs dont elle avait été privée pendant si longtemps. Elle dévorait des yeux la beauté du petit parc qui s'étendait devant elle, le terrain de jeux au delà, la boutique de friandises, la fontaine de pierre et les parterres de fleurs recouverts de neige.

Par dessus les têtes des jeunes spectateurs, elle remarqua un jeune garçon de café qui se tenait debout à l'entrée du petit établissement, en fumant sa cigarette. La princesse le regarda avec admiration et son cœur se mit à battre

✳✳✳✳✳✳✳✳✳✳✳✳✳✳✳✳✳✳✳✳✳✳

Cuando por fin se alzó el telón, la princesa pudo finalmente contemplar el mundo lleno de colores del cual había sido privada por tanto tiempo. Devoraba con los ojos la belleza del pequeño parque que se extendía frente a ellos, el terreno de juegos más allá, la tienda de bocadillos, la fuente de piedra y los cuadros de flores cubiertos de nieve.

Por encima de las cabezas de los pequeños espectadores, reparó en un joven camarero que estaba de pie en la puerta del pequeño café, fumando su cigarrillo. La princesa le miró con admiración y su corazón se puso a palpitar

excitement. She cried out to him, "Help! Save me!" She thrust out her hand in his direction, but the young waiter didn't seem to see it.

Just then the puppeteer reached up and moved the princess to another position on the stage. "Be a good child," he told her. "Don't make such a gloomy face." But she pretended not to hear.

The play began, but the princess could barely follow the action. Spellbound, she glanced again and again at the young man who was watching the puppet show with a smile and seemed to be enjoying it.

✳✳✳✳✳✳✳✳✳✳✳✳✳✳✳✳✳✳✳✳✳✳✳✳

wild zu schlagen. "Hilf mir, rette mich!" rief sie ihm zu und streckte ihm ihre Hand entgegen, doch der Junge schien sie nicht zu sehen.

Der Puppenspieler kam und rückte die Prinzessin zurecht. "Sei ein gutes Kind", ermahnte er sie. "Mach kein so finsteres Gesicht." Doch sie tat, als hätte sie den Meister gar nicht gehört.

Das Spiel begann, doch die Prinzessin folgte dem Geschehen nicht. Sie blickte gebannt hinüber zu dem jungen Mann, der belustigt dem Marionettenspiel zusah.

d'excitation. Elle lui cria: «Au secours! Sauvez-moi!» et tendit la main dans sa direction, mais le jeune garçon de café ne paraissait pas la voir.

Juste à ce moment, le marionnettiste donna à la princesse une nouvelle position sur la scène. «Sois gentille, ma petite fille, lui dit-il, ne fais pas cette tête maussade.» Mais elle fit semblant de ne pas entendre.

La pièce commença, mais la princesse pouvait à peine suivre la scène. Subjuguée, elle lançait sans arrêt des regards vers le jeune homme qui suivait le spectacle de marionnettes en souriant et semblait s'amuser.

✿✿✿✿✿✿✿✿✿✿✿✿✿✿✿✿✿✿✿✿✿

de excitación. Le gritó al joven: —¡Socorro! ¡Sálvame! —y extendió la mano en su dirección, pero el joven no pareció verla.

En ese momento, el titiritero movió a la princesa en otra posición sobre el escenario. —Sé buena niña —le dijo—. No pongas una cara tan hosca. —Pero ésta fingió no haber oído.

Empezó la función, pero la princesa apenas podía seguir la acción. Embelesada, lanzaba miradas una y otra vez hacia el joven y apuesto camarero que estaba mirando el espectáculo de títeres con una sonrisa y parecía divertirse.

"Save me!" she again implored, her arms reaching out to him. The next moment, she felt the pull: the master wanted her to turn toward the prince. I hate this play, the princess thought to herself. I hate my partners, I hate the master. And most of all, she hated her existence. Her only hope, she decided, lay over there with the unknown young man.

Again, she turned toward him, without noticing how the master was directing her movements. Soon her arms and legs became hopelessly entangled in the strings. The

✳✳✳✳✳✳✳✳✳✳✳✳✳✳✳✳✳✳✳✳✳✳

"Rette mich!" flehte sie wieder und streckte die Arme nach ihm aus. Im nächsten Augenblick verspürte sie den Ruck, mit dem der Meister sie dem Prinzen zuwenden wollte. Ich hasse dieses Spiel, dachte sich die Prinzessin. Ich hasse meine Partner, ich hasse den Meister. Vor allem aber hasste sie ihr Dasein. Ihre Rettung, das wusste sie, lag dort drüben bei dem unbekannten Menschen.

Wieder wandte sie sich ihm zu, ohne darauf zu achten, wie der Meister sie lenkte. Bald waren die Führungsstricke ihrer Arme und Beine hoffnungslos verknotet, und der

«Sauvez-moi!» implora-t-elle à nouveau, tendant les bras vers lui. A cet instant, elle sentit l'impulsion du maître qui voulait la faire tourner vers le prince. Je déteste cette pièce, se dit la princesse. Je déteste mes partenaires, je déteste le maître. Et surtout, elle détestait son existence. Son seul espoir, décida-t-elle, reposait là-bas, sur le jeune inconnu.

Elle se tourna de nouveau vers lui, sans se préoccuper de la manière dont le maître dirigeait ses mouvements. Rapidement, ses bras et jambes s'emmêlèrent inextricablement dans les ficelles. Le maître lui lança un regard

✳✳✳✳✳✳✳✳✳✳✳✳✳✳✳✳✳✳✳

—¡Sálvame! —imploró ella de nuevo, alargando los brazos hacia él. Acto seguido, sintió un tirón del amo que quería volverla hacia el príncipe. «Odio esa obra —se dijo la princesa—, odio a mis compañeros, odio al amo.» Más que todo, odiaba su existencia. Su única esperanza, decidió, estaba puesta allá, en el muchacho desconocido.

Se volvió otra vez hacia él, sin fijarse como el amo la animaba. De pronto los hilos que dirigían sus brazos y sus piernas se enredaron sin remedio. El amo le lanzó una

master glowered as he removed her from the play. Without a word he placed her near the edge of the table, then steered the other puppets through the performance.

The princess, though, thought only of her escape. She looked beyond the edge of the table to the ground far below. She felt very scared, but knew there was no other way. She had to jump if she were to gain her freedom.

Quietly she made her way to the rim of the table. Then, closing her eyes, she leaned forward. The drop was dizzying and seemed to take forever. Fortunately she

✳✳✳✳✳✳✳✳✳✳✳✳✳✳✳✳✳✳✳✳✳✳✳

Meister musste die Puppe aus dem Spiel nehmen. Wortlos legte er sie an den Rand des Tisches, während er die anderen Puppen durch das Spiel lenkte.

Die Prinzessin aber dachte nur an ihre Flucht. Über den Rand des Tisches blickte sie hinunter in die Tiefe. Sie hatte grosse Angst, doch gab es keinen anderen Weg. Sie musste sich zu Boden fallen lassen, um ihre Freiheit zu erlangen.

Unauffällig schob sie sich an die Kante des Tisches. Dann schloss sie die Augen und setzte zum Sprung an. Der tiefe Fall war schwindelerregend und schien ohne

courroucé et l'enleva de la pièce. Sans un mot, il la posa au bord de la table, puis continua à manœuvrer les autres marionnettes jusqu'à la fin de la représentation.

La princesse, quant à elle, ne pensait qu'à s'échapper. Elle regarda au-delà du rebord de la table, vers le sol, loin en-dessous. Elle était très effrayée mais savait qu'il n'existait pas d'autre moyen. Il fallait qu'elle saute si elle voulait la liberté.

Tout doucement, elle s'approcha du bord de la table. Alors, en fermant les yeux, elle s'élança en avant. La chute fut vertigineuse et lui sembla durer une éternité. Heureuse-

✳✳✳✳✳✳✳✳✳✳✳✳✳✳✳✳✳✳✳✳✳✳✳

mirada de ira y la sacó de la escena. Sin decir una palabra, la puso cerca del borde de la mesa y manejó a los otros títeres para seguir con la representación.

En cuanto a la princesa, ella solo pensaba en escapar. Miró más allá de la extremidad de la mesa, hacia el suelo, allá abajo. Sintió mucho miedo, pero sabía que no había otro modo. Tenía que saltar si quería lograr su libertad.

Avanzó despacio hasta el borde de la mesa, y cerrando los ojos, se echó adelante. La caída fue vertiginosa y le pareció durar una eternidad. Afortunadamente aterrizó en

landed in the branches of a bush. For a moment she lay there, dazed. Then she tried to wriggle her hands and feet. Nothing seemed to be broken. But how would she get away from here, she wondered.

As she looked around for an answer, she suddenly heard the applause of the children. They were cheering loudly. It no longer seemed important to her. She had given up her success for her freedom.

As the children returned to their games in the park, a little girl came running around the bush. The princess spotted her and quickly tossed her tiny white satin shoe

✳✳✳✳✳✳✳✳✳✳✳✳✳✳✳✳✳✳✳✳✳✳✳

Ende. Glücklicherweise landete sie in den Zweigen eines Busches. Sie blieb vorerst wie betäubt liegen, dann versuchte sie ihre Arme und Beine zu bewegen. Nichts schien gebrochen zu sein. Doch wie würde sie von hier fortkommen, überlegte sie.

Während sie suchend um sich blickte, hörte sie das Klatschen der Kinder. Sie jubelten vor Begeisterung. Doch ihr bedeutete es nichts mehr. Gerne gab sie den Erfolg für ihre Freiheit auf.

Die Kinder kehrten zu ihren Spielen zurück. Ein kleines Mädchen lief um den Busch herum. Als die Prinzessin sie herankommen sah, warf sie ganz schnell ihren

ment, elle atterrit dans les branches d'un buisson. Elle resta là un moment, étourdie. Puis elle essaya de remuer ses mains et ses pieds. Rien ne semblait être cassé. Mais comment pourrait-elle partir de là? se demanda-t-elle.

Alors qu'elle réfléchissait, elle entendit soudain les applaudissements des enfants. Ils manifestaient bruyamment leur joie. Mais cela n'avait plus d'importance pour elle. Elle avait abandonné le succès pour la liberté.

Tandis que les enfants retournaient à leurs jeux dans le parc, une petite fille vint courir autour du buisson. La princesse l'aperçut et lança aussitôt sur la terre gelée son

****

las ramas de un arbusto. Allí se quedó un momento, aturdida. Luego procuró menear las manos y los pies. Nada parecía roto. Pero, ¿como podría irse de aquí? se preguntó.

Mientras buscaba una respuesta a su alrededor, oyó de pronto los aplausos de los niños. Manifestaban su alegría ruidosamente. Pero esto ya no le parecía importante. Había abandonado el éxito por la libertad.

Mientras los niños regresaban a sus juegos en el parque, una chiquilla llegó corriendo alrededor del arbusto. La princesa la vio, y proyectó en seguida su diminuto

onto the frozen ground, right in front of the little girl's feet.

"Look!" The little girl stopped, bent down and picked up the shoe. Her eyes grew wide as she examined it, turning it over and over. Then she peered beneath the bush, hoping to find the other shoe. Suddenly, she saw the princess.

For a moment, the little girl hesitated. Then she reached for the puppet, concealed it under her apron and raced across the playground toward the little cafe. As she burst inside, the proprietress looked up.

✳✳✳✳✳✳✳✳✳✳✳✳✳✳✳✳✳✳✳✳

kleinen, weissen Satinschuh auf den gefrorenen Boden, genau vor die Füsse des Mädchens.

Das Kind hielt inne, bückte sich und hob den Schuh auf. Verwundert betrachtete die Kleine ihren Fund von allen Seiten. Dann kroch sie suchend unter den Busch, in der Hoffnung, den zweiten Schuh zu finden. Plötzlich entdeckte sie die Prinzessin.

Das Kind zögerte einen Augenblick. Dann ergriff es die Puppe, versteckte sie unter seiner Schürze und lief über den Spielplatz zu dem kleinen Kaffeehaus hinüber. Als die Kleine hereinstürzte, hob die Wirtin kurz den Kopf.

minuscule soulier de satin blanc, juste aux pieds de la petite fille.

«Regarde!» La petite fille s'arrêta, se pencha et ramassa le soulier. Elle l'examina dans tous les sens, les yeux écarquillés. Puis elle chercha sous le buisson, espérant trouver l'autre soulier. Soudain, elle aperçut la princesse.

Pendant un instant, la petite fille hésita. Puis elle attrapa la marionnette, la dissimula sous son tablier et traversa le terrain de jeux en courant vers le petit café. Comme elle se précipitait à l'intérieur, la propriétaire leva les yeux.

****

zapato de satén blanco sobre la tierra helada, justo delante de los pies de la niña.

—¡Mira! —La niña se detuvo, se agachó y recogió el zapato. Lo examinó volviéndolo con curiosidad. Luego buscó debajo del arbusto, esperando encontrar el otro zapato. Vio de repente a la princesa.

La niña dudó un instante. Luego recogió la marioneta, la disimuló debajo de su delantal y se fue corriendo hacia el pequeño café, cruzando el terreno de juegos. Como se precipitaba al interior, la propietaria levantó los ojos.

"So you finally got here!" she scolded. "I've called you three times." Without waiting for a reply, she turned her attention to the coffee maker.

The little girl sat down at a table in the darkest corner of the cafe. She glanced around cautiously, then took out the puppet. "You are my guest," she told the princess. "You may order your drink from me—coffee, tea or chocolate?" From a nearby table, the little girl fetched a small pitcher of cream. She poured a few drops into a drinking glass. Then she started to feed the puppet.

✳✳✳✳✳✳✳✳✳✳✳✳✳✳✳✳✳✳✳✳✳

"Endlich bist du wieder da!" schalt sie das Mädchen. "Ich habe dich schon dreimal gerufen." Ohne eine weitere Antwort abzuwarten, wandte sie sich dann wieder der Kaffeemaschine zu.

Das kleine Mädchen setzte sich in der dunkelsten Ecke des Lokals an einen Tisch. Sie schaute verstohlen um sich und holte dann die Puppe hervor. "Du bist mein Gast", sagte sie zur Prinzessin. "Du kannst bei mir bestellen, was du trinken möchtest - Kaffee, Tee oder Schokolade?" Von einem der benachbarten Tische holte das Mädchen ein Kännchen Milch. Sie schüttete etwas davon in ein Glas und begann die Puppe zu füttern.

«Te voilà enfin! gronda-t-elle, je t'ai appelée trois fois.» Sans attendre de réponse, elle se mit à s'occuper de la machine à café.

La petite fille s'assit à une table, dans le coin le plus sombre du café. Elle jeta un coup d'œil autour d'elle, méfiante, puis sortit la marionnette. «Tu es mon hôte, dit-elle à la princesse, tu peux commander une boisson — café, thé ou chocolat?» Sur une table voisine, la petite fille prit un petit pot de crème. Elle en versa quelques gouttes dans un verre puis elle fit boire la marionnette.

✱✱✱✱✱✱✱✱✱✱✱✱✱✱✱✱✱✱✱✱✱

—¡Por fin has llegado! —la regañó—. Te he llamado tres veces. —Sin esperar una respuesta, se volvió hacia la máquina de café.

La niña se sentó en una mesa en el rincón más oscuro del café. Echó una mirada prudente alrededor, y sacó la marioneta. —Eres mi convidada —le dijo a la princesa—. Puedes pedirme una bebida, ¿café, té, o chocolate? —Sobre una mesa cercana, cogió un pequeño jarro de crema. Echó unas gotas en un vaso y dio de beber a la marioneta.

This wasn't exactly what the princess had hoped for. But, at least she was proving she could get along without the master. Sullenly, she tossed her head back, and the little girl spilled cream upon the puppet's dress.

Ordinarily, the princess would have been annoyed by this, but just then her attention was diverted by the sound of loud voices coming from the entrance. One of them, she realized, was her master's voice, and she began to tremble with excitement.

✳✳✳✳✳✳✳✳✳✳✳✳✳✳✳✳✳✳✳✳✳✳

Das war nicht gerade, was die Prinzessin sich erhofft hatte. Doch immerhin hatte sie bewiesen, dass sie auch ohne den Meister zurechtkommen konnte. Trotzig warf sie den Kopf in den Nacken, und das Kind verschüttete Milch auf das schöne, rosa Kleid.

Normalerweise wäre die Prinzessin darüber verärgert gewesen, doch wurde ihre Aufmerksamkeit von lautem Stimmengewirr in Anspruch genommen, das vom Eingang her zu ihr klang. Sie erkannte die Stimme des Meisters sofort und begann vor Erregung zu zittern.

Ce n'était pas exactement ce que la princesse avait espéré, mais au moins, elle prouvait qu'elle était capable de se débrouiller sans le maître. De mauvaise grâce, elle rejeta la tête en arrière et l'enfant renversa de la crème sur la robe de la marionnette.

D'ordinaire, la princesse en aurait été contrariée, mais juste à ce moment-là son attention fut attirée par un bruit de voix élevées provenant de l'entrée. Elle reconnut immédiatement celle de son maître, et se mit à trembler d'excitation.

✳✳✳✳✳✳✳✳✳✳✳✳✳✳✳✳✳✳✳✳✳✳✳

Esto no era exactamente lo que había esperado la princesa. Pero por lo menos, estaba demostrando que podía arreglárselas sin el amo. Obstinada, echó la cabeza para atrás y la niña virtió crema en el vestido rosado de la marioneta.

De ordinario, ello hubiera molestado a la princesa, pero en este momento su atención fue desviada por el ruido de voces fuertes que procedían de la entrada. Reconoció inmediatamente la voz de su amo y se puso a temblar de excitación.

"I want my puppet back," the old man shouted. "Somebody stole her!" But the proprietress blocked the entrance with her massive body and snapped, "You have a lot of nerve, you vagabond! First, you snatch away all of my customers with your performance and then you accuse us of stealing. I'll get the police after you, you old tramp!"

But the showman didn't budge. "Your daughter was seen picking up the puppet," he said. "The children in the park told me she ran in here carrying it. Please give me back my puppet," he implored. "It is my finest piece."

✳✳✳✳✳✳✳✳✳✳✳✳✳✳✳✳✳✳✳✳✳✳

"Ich will meine Puppe zurückhaben", schrie der alte Mann. "Man hat sie mir gestohlen!" Doch die Wirtin, die mit der Masse ihres Körpers die ganze Türöffnung füllte, fauchte drohend zurück: "Was erlaubst du dir, du Vagabund! Zuerst schnappst du mir mit deiner Vorstellung alle Gäste weg, und dann versuchst du noch, uns zu beschuldigen. Die Polizei werde ich dir auf den Hals jagen, du Strolch!"

Doch der Schausteller liess sich nicht abweisen. In flehendem Ton fuhr er fort: "Man hat gesehen, dass deine Tochter die Puppe aufgeklaubt hat. Die Kinder im Park haben mir gesagt, dass sie damit hierher gelaufen ist. Bitte, gib mir die Puppe zurück. Sie ist mein bestes Stück."

«Je veux ma marionnette», criait le vieil homme. «Quelqu'un l'a volée!» Mais la propriétaire bloqua l'entrée de sa silhouette massive et répliqua: «Vous en avez du toupet, vagabond! D'abord vous m'enlevez tous mes clients avec votre spectacle, et ensuite vous nous accusez d'avoir volé, nous! Je vais appeler la police, vieux clochard!»

Mais le forain ne bougeait pas. «Votre fille a été vue en train de ramasser la marionnette, dit-il, les enfants du parc m'ont dit qu'elle l'a emportée ici en courant. S'il vous plaît, rendez-moi ma marionnette, supplia-t-il, c'est ma plus belle pièce!»

✱✱✱✱✱✱✱✱✱✱✱✱✱✱✱✱✱✱✱✱✱✱✱

—¡Quiero mi marioneta! —gritaba el viejo hombre—. ¡Me la ha robado alguien! —Pero la propietaria bloqueó la entrada con su cuerpo masivo y replicó:

—¡Qué descaro el tuyo, vagabundo! Primero me quitas todos mis clientes con tu teatro, y luego nos acusas a nosotras de haber robado. Voy a llamar a la policía, ¡viejo mendigo!

Pero el saltimbanqui no se movió. —Han visto a su hija recogiendo a la marioneta, —dijo él—. Los niños del parque me han dicho que ha venido corriendo hasta aquí llevándosela. Por favor, devuélvanme mi marioneta —imploró—. Es mi pieza más preciosa.

Both the princess and the little girl, huddling together in the dark corner, followed this exchange attentively. At the final words, the little girl jumped up, grabbed the puppet and slipped out of the back door.

At the rear of the building things were in a sorry state. Empty cartons littered the ground and next to a row of overflowing trash cans lay soiled paper napkins and cake crumbs.

"If that child puts me down here, I'll die of disgust,"

✳✳✳✳✳✳✳✳✳✳✳✳✳✳✳✳✳✳✳✳✳✳✳

Nicht nur die Prinzessin, sondern auch das kleine Mädchen, das mit ihr zusammen in der dunklen Ecke hockte, hatte den Wortwechsel aufmerksam verfolgt. Bei den letzten Worten sprang das Kind auf, erwischte die Puppe und schlüpfte durch eine Hintertür ins Freie.

Hier an der Rückseite des Gebäudes sah es schlimm aus. Leere Kartons häuften sich übereinander, und neben einem überquellenden Abfalleimer lagen schmutzige Papierservietten und Küchenreste.

"Wenn mich das Kind hier wegwirft, sterbe ich vor

La princesse et la petite fille, blotties l'une contre l'autre dans le coin sombre, suivaient attentivement cet échange de propos. Après quoi, la petite fille se releva d'un bond, saisit la marionnette et se glissa dehors par la porte de derrière.

Lá, derrière le bâtiment, tout était en piteux état. Des cartons vides jonchaient le sol et des serviettes en papier sales et des miettes de gâteaux traînaient près d'une rangée de poubelles débordantes.

«Si cette enfant me dépose ici, je mourrai de dégoût»

****

La princesa y la niña, apretadas la una contra la otra en el rincón oscuro, seguían esta discusión con atención. Al final la niña saltó de pie, agarró la marioneta y se deslizó por la puerta del fondo.

Allí, detrás del edificio, las cosas estaban en un estado total de abandono. Cajas vacias cubrían el suelo, y junto a una hilera de cubos de basura rebosantes, yacían servilletas de papel y migas de pasteles.

—Si me deja aquí esta niña, me voy a morir de asco—,

the princess grimaced. But the little girl carried her around the corner of the building to a parked car. Quickly, she opened the door and thrust the puppet into the glove compartment. Then the door slammed shut as she raced off to join her friends.

The princess had been stuffed amid a pile of old travel brochures and road maps. The glove compartment smelled of stale cigarettes and beer. She wrinkled her nose. This was not at all what she had expected.

✳✳✳✳✳✳✳✳✳✳✳✳✳✳✳✳✳✳✳✳✳

Ekel", fuhr es der armen Prinzessin durch den Kopf. Doch die Kleine lief um die Ecke zu einem abgestellten Auto. Schnell öffnete sie die Tür und quetschte die Puppe in das Handschuhfach. Dann schlug sie die Tür wieder zu und lief zurück zu ihren Freunden.

Da lag nun die Prinzessin, eingezwängt zwischen alten Prospekten und Landkarten. Es roch nach Zigaretten und Bier. Angewidert rümpfte sie die Nase. Das war auch nicht, was sie erwartet hatte.

se dit en grimaçant la princesse. Mais la petite fille contourna le coin du bâtiment et se dirigea vers une voiture garée là. Elle ouvrit brusquement la portière et jeta la marionnette dans la boîte à gants. Alors la portière se referma violemment et elle partit rejoindre ses amis.

La princesse avait été fourrée au milieu d'une pile de vieilles brochures de voyage et de cartes routières. La boîte à gants sentait la cigarette et la bière éventée. Elle fit la grimace. Ce n'était pas du tout ce qu'elle espérait.

✳✳✳✳✳✳✳✳✳✳✳✳✳✳✳✳✳✳✳✳✳

dijo la princesa con una mueca de disgusto. Pero la niña dio la vuelta de la esquina del edificio y se acercó a un coche aparcado. Rápidamente, abrió la puerta e introdujo la marioneta en la guantera. De un golpe, cerró la puerta del vehículo y se fue corriendo a juntarse con sus amigos.

La princesa había sido metida entre una pila de viejos folletos de viajes y mapas de carreteras. La guantera olía a tabaco viejo y a cerveza. Frunció la nariz. Esto no era en absoluto lo que había esperado.

Hours dragged by before she finally heard footsteps. Then the car door opened and someone slid inside. As the motor started, the puppet began to tremble at the thought of being driven away into the unknown.

As she struggled to regain her composure, a feeling of terror suddenly engulfed her. A man's hand was groping around the glove compartment. She struggled to lay back, making herself as flat as possible to avoid his grasp, but there was not enough room. Suddenly the fingers closed over her shoulder and pulled her out.

✱✱✱✱✱✱✱✱✱✱✱✱✱✱✱✱✱✱✱✱✱

Stunden vergingen, ehe sie Schritte hörte. Die Tür wurde aufgemacht und jemand stieg ein. Der Motor sprang an, und zitternd spürte die Marionette, wie sie ins Unbekannte entführt wurde.

Sie bemühte sich, ihre Gedanken zu sammeln und erschrak gewaltig, als eine Männerhand tastend ins Handschuhfach fuhr. Sie versuchte, sich ganz an die Wand zu drücken, um dem Zugriff zu entgehen, doch der Raum war zu eng. Plötzlich umschlossen die Finger ihre Schultern und zogen sie heraus.

De longues heures passèrent avant qu'elle entende enfin des pas. Alors, la portière de la voiture s'ouvrit, et quelqu'un se glissa à l'interieur. Comme le moteur se mettait en route, la marionnette commença à trembler à la pensée d'être emmenée au loin, vers l'inconnu.

Elle essayait de retrouver son calme mais la terreur l'envahit soudain; une main d'homme tâtonnait dans la boîte à gants. Elle chercha à reculer, en s'aplatissant autant que possible pour éviter la main, mais il n'y avait pas assez de place. Soudain, les doigts se refermèrent sur son épaule et la sortirent.

✳✳✳✳✳✳✳✳✳✳✳✳✳✳✳✳✳✳✳✳✳✳

Pasaron horas hasta que por fin oyó pasos. Entonces, se abrió la puerta del coche y alguien penetró al interior. Al arrancar el motor, la marioneta se puso a temblar a la idea de ser llevada lejos, hacia lo desconocido.

Se esforzaba en recuperar la calma, pero de pronto se sintió sumergida por una sensación de terror cuando una mano de hombre buscó a tientas por la guantera. Intentó echarse para atrás para evitar la mano, pero no había bastante espacio. Súbitamente, los dedos la agarraron por el hombro y la sacaron.

"How in the world did you get in here?" the driver exclaimed in amazement. The car braked to an abrupt halt.

As she looked up at him, the princess felt her fears give way to a rush of happiness. Holding her in both of his hands was none other than her hero, the young man she had begged to help her escape during the performance. At that realization, the princess flushed with embarrassment; she knew she looked messy and unkempt.

"You must forgive my appearance," she begged. "My escape wasn't easy. I even lost a shoe," she added quickly, aware that he was scrutinizing her from head to toe.

✻✻✻✻✻✻✻✻✻✻✻✻✻✻✻✻✻✻✻✻✻

"Wo in aller Welt kommst du denn her?" fragte der Fahrer verblüfft und stieg kräftig auf die Bremse.

Als die kleine Puppe ihn sah, verlor sie alle Angst und war überwältigt von Glück. Der Mann, der sie nun staunend in Händen hielt, war niemand anders als ihr Held, der junge Mann, den sie während der Vorstellung um Hilfe angefleht hatte. Es war ihr nur peinlich, dass sie so unordentlich und zerrauft aussah.

"Du musst meinen Zustand entschuldigen", bat sie. "Meine Flucht war nicht leicht. Mir ist sogar ein Schuh abhanden gekommen", fügte sie erklärend hinzu, da sie sah, wie der Bursch sie von oben bis unten musterte.

«Comment diable es-tu entrèe là-dedans?» s'exclama le conducteur stupéfié. La voiture freina et s'arrêta brusquement.

En levant les yeux vers lui, la princesse oublia sa peur et fut submergée par la joie. Celui qui la tenait dans ses deux mains n'était autre que son héros, le jeune homme qu'elle avait supplié de l'aider à s'enfuir pendant la représentation. A cette pensée, la princesse rougit d'embarras; elle savait qu'elle avait l'air désordonné et était ébouriffée.

«Pardonnez ma tenue, supplia-t-elle, ma fuite n'a pas été aisée. J'ai même perdu un soulier» ajouta-t-elle rapidement, se rendant compte qu'il était en train de l'examiner de la tête aux pieds.

✳✳✳✳✳✳✳✳✳✳✳✳✳✳✳✳✳✳✳✳✳✳✳

—¿Cómo demonios has llegado aquí? —exclamó el conductor, asombrado. El coche frenó bruscamente.

Al mirarle, la princesa sintió que su miedo dejaba sitio a la alegría. El que la tenía en sus dos manos no era otro que su héroe, el joven a quien había rogado que la salvara durante la representación. La princesa se ruborizó de confusión; sabía que parecía desordenada y desgreñada.

—Usted debe perdonar mi aspecto —le rogó—. Mi huída no fue fácil. Hasta perdí un zapato —añadió enseguida, consciente de que la estaba observando de los pies a la cabeza.

His fingers moved over her porcelain face. They were rough fingers, not nearly as soft and gentle as the puppeteer's, and their nails were broken. But that did not matter to her because she loved her hero. She even wanted to hug him, but she knew that would not be proper.

The young man turned her around and around as he examined her. He wanted to put her on the seat next to his but the wires that held her began to get tangled. So he picked her up and without much ado suspended her from the rear view mirror.

✳✳✳✳✳✳✳✳✳✳✳✳✳✳✳✳✳✳✳✳✳✳✳

Seine Finger fuhren über ihr Porzellangesicht. Es waren rauhe Finger, nicht so weiche wie die des Puppenspielers und mit abgebrochenen Nägeln. Doch das spielte ihr keine Rolle, denn sie liebte ihren Retter. Eigentlich wäre sie ihm am liebsten um den Hals gefallen, doch wusste sie, dass sich das nicht schickte.

Der junge Mann drehte die Puppe hin und her, während er sie betrachtete. Er wollte sie auf den Nebensitz legen, doch die Führungsfäden begannen sich zu verwirren. Da hob er sie wieder auf und hängte sie kurzentschlossen am Rückspiegel auf.

Ses doigts effleurèrent sa figure de porcelaine. C'étaient des doigts rêches, loin d'être aussi doux et délicats que ceux du marionnettiste, et leurs ongles étaient cassés. Mais tout cela était sans importance, car elle aimait son héros. Elle voulait même l'embrasser mais elle réalisa que ce ne serait pas convenable.

Le jeune homme la tourna dans tout les sens en l'examinant. Il voulut la poser sur le siège à côté du sien, mais les fils qui l'actionnaient s'emmêlèrent. Alors il la souleva et tout simplement, la suspendit au rétroviseur.

✳✳✳✳✳✳✳✳✳✳✳✳✳✳✳✳✳✳✳✳✳

Los dedos del joven tocaron su cara de porcelana. Eran dedos ásperos, lejos de ser tan suaves y ligeros como los del titiritero, y sus uñas estaban rotas. Pero ello no le importaba porque quería a su héroe. Hasta quería abrazarlo, pero sabía que no sería decente.

El joven la volvió una y otra vez, examinándola. Quiso ponerla en el asiento a su lado, pero los hilos que la sostenían se enredaron. Entonces la cogió y sin más ni más la colgó al retrovisor.

135

As the car cruised through the streets of the town the little princess finally had her long dreamed of chance to see the world. She eyed the gaily-decorated windows of the fine boutiques and the milliner's store and yearned to shop there.

She saw people sitting at tables in the outdoor cafes, laughing and talking, and she wished she could belong to them. Again her wishes seemed to be coming true when the young man suddenly rolled his car to a stop in front of one of the stores where a group of his friends were standing. "Want a ride?" he called out.

✳✳✳✳✳✳✳✳✳✳✳✳✳✳✳✳✳✳✳✳✳✳

Während das Auto nun durch die Strassen der Stadt fuhr, bot sich der kleinen Prinzessin endlich Gelegenheit, die Welt zu sehen. Sie blickte in die Auslagen der Modesalons und Hutgeschäfte und sehnte sich danach, dort einzukaufen.

Sie sah lachende Menschen in reger Unterhaltung an den vor den Kaffeehäusern aufgestellten Tischen sitzen und wünschte, dazuzugehören. Wieder schienen ihre Wünsche in Erfüllung zu gehen, denn der Mann hielt sein Auto vor einem der Lokale an und lud ein paar Freunde, die dort standen, zum Mitfahren ein.

Tandis que la voiture parcourait les rues de la ville, la petite princesse avait enfin la chance longtemps rêvée de voir le monde. Elle découvrait les vitrines des belles boutiques gaiement décorées, le magasin de la modiste, et mourait d'envie d'y aller faire des emplettes.

Elle voyait les gens assis aux tables des terrasses de café, qui riaient et qui bavardaient, et elle aurait bien aimé être avec eux. Ses espoirs furent de nouveau sur le point de se réaliser quand le jeune homme arrêta soudain sa voiture en face d'un des magasins où se tenait un groupe de ses amis. «Je peux vous amener quelque part?» leur cria-t-il.

✿✿✿✿✿✿✿✿✿✿✿✿✿✿✿✿✿✿✿✿✿✿

Mientras el coche recorría las calles de la ciudad, la pequeña princesa tenía por fin la oportunidad que había soñado tanto tiempo, la de ver el mundo. Admiraba los escaparates alegremente adornados de las tiendas finas, del almacén de la modista de sombreros, y tenía ganas de ir de compras.

Veía gente sentada en las mesas de las terrazas de los cafés que reía y charlaba, y hubiera querido estar con ella. Sus deseos otra vez parecieron hacerse realidad cuando el joven paró su coche enfrente de una tienda donde estaba un grupo de amigos suyos. —¿Os llevo? —les gritó.

The moment they climbed into the car one of them noticed the princess. "Where did you pick up this doll?" he asked.

"A very classy lady," said another. "And she'll never talk back to you."

"We never knew you hobnobbed with fancy people," teased a third. "Hey, let me take a look at her, will you?"

With that, the young man sitting in the front passenger seat took down the puppet and handed her to his friends. They weren't exactly gentle as they passed her around. This was very unpleasant for the princess and she began to sob.

✳✳✳✳✳✳✳✳✳✳✳✳✳✳✳✳✳✳✳✳✳✳

Kaum waren sie eingestiegen, so bemerkte einer von ihnen die Prinzessin. "Wo hast du denn diese Puppe aufgegabelt?" fragte er.

"Eine sehr vornehme Dame", sagte ein anderer. "Und noch dazu eine, die nie widerspricht."

"Wir wussten gar nicht, dass du in so vornehmen Kreisen verkehrst", hänselte ihn ein Dritter. "Lass mich sie auch ansehen."

Mit diesen Worten nahm der neben dem Fahrer sitzende Mann die Puppe herunter und reichte sie seinen Freunden weiter. Während die Prinzessin herumgereicht wurde, gingen sie nicht gerade zart mit ihr um. Das war ihr sehr unangenehm, und sie begann zu schluchzen.

Au moment où ils montaient dans la voiture, l'un d'eux remarqua la princesse. «Où as-tu ramassé cette poupée?» demanda-t-il.

«Une dame de grande classe, dit un autre, et qui ne sera jamais impertinente avec toi.»

«On ne savait pas que tu fréquentais des gens chics, plaisanta un troisième, eh, laisse-moi lui jeter un coup d'œil, d'accord?»

A ces mots, le jeune homme assis sur le siège du passager avant détacha la marionnette et la passa à ses amis. Ils n'étaient pas très délicats en se la passant de l'un à l'autre. Ceci déplut fort à la princesse et elle se mit à sangloter.

✳✳✳✳✳✳✳✳✳✳✳✳✳✳✳✳✳✳✳✳✳✳✳✳

Al subir en el coche, uno de ellos se fijó en la princesa. —¿De dónde has sacado esta muñeca? —preguntó.

—Una dama de mucha categoría —dijo otro—. Y que no va a reñir nunca.

—No sabíamos que tratabas con gente distinguida, —bromeó un tercero—. ¡Eh! déjame echarle un ojo ¿de acuerdo?

Al oír estas palabras, el joven sentado en el asiento delantero del pasajero descolgó la marioneta y la dio a sus amigos. No eran muy delicados al pasársela uno a otro. Esto era muy desagradable para la princesa y se puso a sollozar.

"Please stop them!" she begged of her rescuer. "I love and trust you because you saved me. But your friends are very coarse and rough. Look how they're tossing me around—and soiling my fine clothes with their dirty fingers."

But her hero didn't answer. He merely smiled at their remarks, even if he seemed a bit embarrassed and annoyed by their teasing.

His friends, however, didn't let up. Instead, their crass comments about him and the puppet became more and more vulgar. At last the driver grew really angry. Whirling around, he jerked the puppet from his friends' hands and hurled it out the window.

✳✳✳✳✳✳✳✳✳✳✳✳✳✳✳✳✳✳✳✳✳

"Lass das bitte nicht zu!" flehte sie ihren Retter an. Du kannst von mir verlangen, was du willst, denn du hast mich gerettet. Aber deine Freunde sind derb und grob. Schau, wie sie mich herumstossen und mit ihren schmutzigen Händen meine Kleider ganz fleckig machen!"

Doch ihr Held gab keine Antwort. Er lachte nur geniert und schien sich über die Neckerei seiner Freunde zu ärgern.

Die jedoch liessen nicht davon ab. Ihre Anspielungen auf ihn und die Puppe wurden im Gegenteil immer gewöhnlicher. Da wurde der Fahrer wirklich böse. Er kurbelte das Fenster herunter, riss den Freunden die Puppe aus der Hand und schleuderte sie in grossem Bogen aus dem Fenster.

«S'il te plaît, arrête-les!» implora-t-elle de son sauveur. «Je t'aime et te fais confiance parce que tu m'as sauvée. Mais tes amis sont très grossiers et très brutaux. Regarde comme ils me secouent et salissent mes beaux habits avec leurs doigts sales.»

Mais son héros ne répondit pas. Il se contentait de sourire à leurs propos, bien qu'il parût un peu gêné et ennuyé par leurs plaisanteries.

Cependant, ses amis n'arrêtaient pas. Au contraire, leurs réflexions stupides sur lui et la marionnette devinrent de plus en plus vulgaires. A la fin, le conducteur se fâcha vraiment. Il se retourna, arracha la marionnette des mains de ses amis et la lança par la fenêtre.

✳✳✳✳✳✳✳✳✳✳✳✳✳✳✳✳✳✳✳✳✳✳

—Por favor, ¡ deténles! —le suplicó a su salvador—. Te quiero y confío en ti porque me has salvado. Pero tus amigos son muy groseros y violentos. Mira como me están revolviendo y manchando la ropa con sus dedos sucios.

Pero su héroe no contestó. Solo sonreía por los comentarios de ellos, aunque parecía un poco incómodo y fastidiado por sus bromas.

Pero sus amigos no pararon. Al contrario, sus comentarios estúpidos acerca de él y de la marioneta se hicieron más y más vulgares. Al fin, el conductor terminó verdaderamente enojado. Volviéndose, arrancó la marioneta de las manos de sus amigos y la arrojó por la ventana.

141

This took place so fast that the princess didn't have time to realize what had happened until after the dust had cleared from the departing car. She lay in a ditch by the side of the road next to a rusty tin can, her limbs badly bruised, her clothing torn.

As time passed, rain and snow caused her to sink ever more deeply into the soft earth. Soon, it enclosed her almost like grave. She could not hear the dragging footsteps of the old puppeteer as he wandered along the streets of the town with his suitcase, brokenhearted, searching for his best piece, the lost princess.

✳✳✳✳✳✳✳✳✳✳✳✳✳✳✳✳✳✳✳✳✳✳✳

Das alles ereignete sich so schnell, dass die Prinzessin überhaupt nicht erfasste, was geschah. Sie kam erst wieder zur Besinnung, als der Staub des davonfahrenden Autos sich auf der Strasse gesetzt hatte. Sie lag im Strassengraben neben einer rostigen Konserve, zerschunden und zerrissen.

Regen und Schnee liessen sie immer tiefer im weichen Erdreich versinken wie in einem Grab, und sie hörte nicht mehr die schlurfenden Schritte des Puppenspielers, der gebrochen mit seinem Koffer die Strassen entlangirrte und nach seinem besten Stück Ausschau hielt.

Tout se passa si vite que la princesse n'eut pas le temps de se rendre compte de ce qui était arrivé jusqu'à ce que la poussière, soulevée par le départ de la voiture, se soit dissipée. Elle gisait là, dans un fossé au bord de la route, à côté d'une boîte de conserves rouillée, les membres tout meurtris, les vêtements déchirés.

La pluie et la neige la firent s'enfoncer encore plus profondément dans la terre molle. Elle la recouvrit bientôt presque comme une tombe, ce qui l'empêcha d'entendre les pas traînants du vieux marionnettiste qui errait le long des rues de la ville, le cœur brisé, sa valise à la main, à la recherche de sa plus belle pièce.

✳✳✳✳✳✳✳✳✳✳✳✳✳✳✳✳✳✳✳✳✳✳✳

Todo eso sucedió tan rápido que la princesa soló pudo darse cuenta de lo que había sucedido después de disipado el polvo levantado por el coche que se alejaba. Allí yacía, en una cuneta a un lado de la carretera, junto a una lata enmohecida, con los miembros muy contusionados y la ropa desgarrada.

La lluvia y la nieve la hicieron hundirse más y más profundamente en la tierra blanda. Pronto, esta la cubrió casi como una tumba, impidiéndole que oyera los pasos del viejo titiritero que iba con su maleta, arrastrando los pies por las calles de la ciudad, con el corazón quebrado, buscando su mejor pieza.

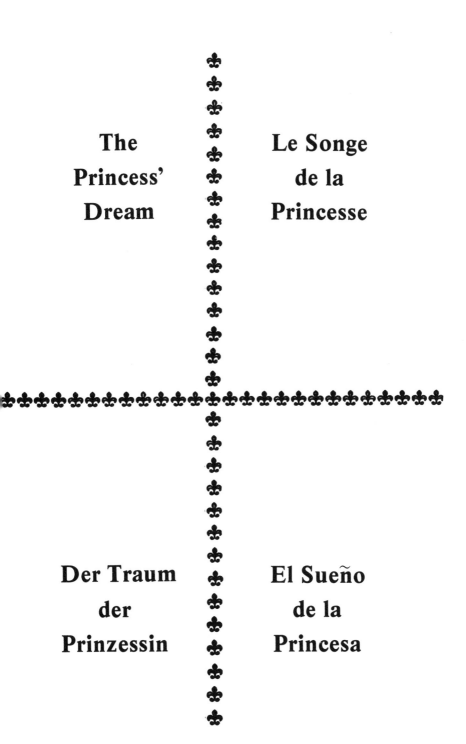

The
Princess'
Dream

Le Songe
de la
Princesse

Der Traum
der
Prinzessin

El Sueño
de la
Princesa

Strictly speaking, she was not really a princess at all. Nor did she fit the image of a princess. She was not slender and delicate but robust, not fair but suntanned. Still, she lived in an old castle situated high over the valley and had been called Princess almost from the day she was born.

A steep and rocky road led from the village up to this citadel, built upon a rugged cliff. Day in and day out hordes of visitors hiked up to tour the castle.

The princess's father would open the massive wooden

Genaugenommen war sie gar keine echte Prinzessin. Auch ihr Aussehen entsprach nicht dem Bild einer Prinzessin. Sie war nicht feingliedrig, sondern kräftig gebaut, nicht blass, sondern sonnengebräunt. Doch wohnte sie in einer alten Burg, hoch oben über dem Tal und wurde von klein auf Prinzessin gerufen.

Ein steiler, steiniger Weg führte vom Dorf hinauf zu der Festung, die auf einem schroffen Felsen errichtet war. Tagaus, tagein wanderten Besucher hinauf, um die Burg zu besichtigen.

Der Vater der Prinzessin öffnete die riesigen, schweren

A vrai dire, elle n'était pas du tout princesse. Elle ne correspondait pas non plus à l'image d'une princesse. Elle n'était pas mince et fine, mais solide, non pas de teint pâle, mais hâlée par le soleil. Cependant elle vivait dans un vieux château qui dominait la vallée et on l'appelait Princesse depuis qu'elle était petite.

Du village, une route escarpée et caillouteuse menait à cette citadelle bâtie au sommet d'une falaise abrupte. Jour après jour, des visiteurs effectuaient la montée pour se rendre au château.

Le père de la princesse ouvrait le portail en bois massif

A decir verdad, no era realmente una princesa. Tampoco correspondía a la imagen de una princesa. No era fina y delicada, de tez pálida, sino robusta y bronceada. Sin embargo, vivía en un castillo antiguo que dominaba el valle y la llamaban Princesa desde pequeña.

Una carretera empinada y pedregosa conducía del pueblo a esta ciudadela edificada en lo alto de un acantilado abrupto. Cada día subían visitantes a ver el castillo.

El padre de la princesa abría los portales de madera

entrance doors and guide the visitors up and down through the inner courts, the halls and chambers, the dungeon, the peel towers, recounting the stormy events that had taken place there.

But during these tours the princess would run down to the village. She could not stand having strangers in her castle. She preferred instead to help the town seamstress with her sewing, the farmers' wives with their milking, the local children with their lessons. Everyone was glad to see her, and if she failed to show up one day, they would ask her the next:

Holztore und führte die Besucher durch die Höfe, die Säle und Kammern, Verliese, die Wehrtürme treppauf, treppab und schilderte ihnen die wechselhaften Ereignisse, die sich hier zugetragen hatten.

Die Prinzessin aber lief währenddessen ins Dorf hinunter. Sie sah Fremde in ihrer Burg gar nicht gern. Lieber half sie der Schneiderin beim Nähen, den Bäuerinnen beim Melken, den Kindern bei ihren Aufgaben. Jedermann freute sich über ihr Kommen, und blieb sie einmal aus, so fragte man sie tags darauf:

et guidait les visiteurs de bas en haut, à travers cours intérieures, grandes salles et chambres diverses, le donjon, les tours de garde, tout en racontant les événements tumultueux dont ils avaient été les témoins.

Mais pendant ces visites, la princesse descendait en courant au village. Elle n'aimait pas la présence d'étrangers dans son château et préférait aider la couturière à sa couture, traire les vaches avec les fermières ou aider les enfants à faire leurs devoirs. Tout le monde était heureux de la voir, et si un jour on ne la voyait pas, on lui demandait le lendemain :

maciza y guiaba los visitantes por los patios interiores, las salas y las habitaciones, las torres desconchadas, la torre del homenaje, de arriba abajo, mientras contaba los acontecimientos atormentados que ocurrieron allí.

Pero la princesa bajaba corriendo al pueblo. No soportaba a los extranjeros en su castillo. Prefería ayudar a la costurera con su labor, a las granjeras con el ordeño y a los niños con sus deberes. Todos estaban contentos de verla, y si algún día no acudía, le preguntaban el día siguiente:

"Princess, where were you yesterday? We missed you."

In the afternoon the princess would run home again, once the last train had chugged out of the small village station bearing away the visitors, and the dust raised by their departing cars had settled again on the quiet country road.

She would dart past her parents' gate house, slip into the castle through a decaying wooden door and patter down into the enormous kitchen, whose walls were lined with pewter plates and mugs. Here she would turn the old,

❦❦❦❦❦❦❦❦❦❦❦❦❦❦❦❦❦❦❦❦❦❦❦❦

"Wo warst du gestern, Prinzessin? Wir haben auf dich gewartet."

Am Nachmittag, wenn der letzte Zug den kleinen Dorfbahnhof schnaufend verlassen hatte, wenn der Staub der Autos, welche die fremden Besucher wegbrachten, sich wieder auf der einsamen Landstrasse gesetzt hatte, kehrte die Prinzessin nach Hause zurück.

Unbemerkt huschte sie am Pförtnerhaus der Eltern vorbei, schlüpfte durch eine vermorschte Holztür in die Burg und stieg in die riesige Küche hinab, an deren Wänden die Zinnkrüge und Teller aufgereiht standen. Sie drehte den

«Princesse, où était-tu hier? Tu nous as manqué!»

La princesse retournait au château l'après-midi, après le départ du dernier train de la petite gare du village, dès que la poussière soulevée par les voitures emmenant les étrangers était retombée sur la route déserte.

Elle passait vite devant la maison des gardiens où vivaient ses parents, se faufilait à l'intérieur du château par une porte de bois vermoulu, et descendait dans l'immense cuisine, dont les murs étaient garnis de chopes d'étain et

⚜⚜⚜⚜⚜⚜⚜⚜⚜⚜⚜⚜⚜⚜⚜⚜⚜⚜⚜⚜⚜

—Princesa, ¿dónde estabas ayer? Te echamos de menos.

Por la tarde, la princesa regresaba corriendo al castillo, después de haber salido el último tren de la estación del pequeño pueblo, y de haber recaído sobre la carretera rural desierta el polvo levantado por los coches que se llevaban a los extranjeros.

Pasó rápido delante de la casa de guarda de sus padres, se coló al interior del castillo por una puerta de madera carcomida, y bajó taconeando a la cocina enorme cuyas paredes estaban adornadas con platos y jarras de estaño.

rusty spit that could hold a whole boar for roasting over the flames below.

She could just imagine what a bustle there must have been down here when the great hall resounded with festivities. She could almost see the young kitchen boys who had run upstairs with the steaming bowls of food, bumping into the servant girls returning with dirty dishes, and the old cellarman panting as he lugged the brimming jugs of wine up the stairs, stopping halfway to catch his breath and to take a hefty sip himself.

⚜⚜⚜⚜⚜⚜⚜⚜⚜⚜⚜⚜⚜⚜⚜⚜⚜⚜⚜⚜

alten, rostigen Spiess, der einen ganzen Eber über dem Feuer rösten konnte.

Sie konnte sich ganz genau vorstellen, was für ein Getümmel hier unten geherrscht haben musste, wenn oben im Saal gefeiert wurde. Sie sah förmlich die Küchenjungen, die mit dampfenden Schüsseln hinauflaufen mussten und auf den engen Stiegen mit den Mägden zusammenstiessen, die das schmutzige Tafelgeschirr wegtrugen, und den alten Kellermeister, der keuchend die vollen Weinkrüge hinaufschleppte, und mitten am Weg vor lauter Erschöpfung innehielt und selber einen kräftigen Schluck nahm.

d'assiettes. Elle faisait tourner la vieille broche rouillée qui pouvait faire rôtir un sanglier tout entier.

Elle pouvait facilement imaginer l'affairement qui avait dû régner quand les fêtes se déroulaient dans la grande salle. Elle imaginait les garçons de cuisine qui devaient monter en courant les escaliers en portant des récipients fumants, se heurtant aux servantes qui, elles, redescendaient chargées de vaisselle sale, et au vieux sommelier qui, haletant, portait les cruches de vin pleines à ras bord, s'arrêtant à mi-chemin pour reprendre son souffle et avaler lui-même une bonne lampée.

❖❖❖❖❖❖❖❖❖❖❖❖❖❖❖❖❖❖❖❖❖❖❖

Hizo girar el viejo espetón enmohecido que podía asar un jabalí entero.

Podía imaginar fácilmente cuánto ajetreo habría aquí abajo cuando resonaron los ruidos de festejos en la sala grande. Casi podía ver a los mozos de cocina que subían rápidamente las escaleras con las fuentes humeantes, tropezando con las sirvientas que traían la vajilla sucia, y con el viejo botillero que cargaba, jadeante, los jarros de vino, parándose a medio camino para recobrar el aliento y tomar él mismo un buen trago.

At this the princess had to laugh. Then she would race up the narrow stairway that led to the banquet hall. Here she snuggled into one of the oriels on a carved wooden bench and surveyed the richly-woven banners that waited to be waved once again.

The setting sun bathed the room in a reddish-gold light, and to the princess it seemed the logs on the open hearth might even begin to crackle.

The cozy warmth made the hall come alive, and as she stared up dreamily at the dark, venerable paintings, the

⚜⚜⚜⚜⚜⚜⚜⚜⚜⚜⚜⚜⚜⚜⚜⚜⚜⚜⚜⚜

Über diese Vorstellung musste die Prinzessin selbst lachen. Schnell lief sie die enge Treppe hinauf, die zum Festsaal führte. Hier kuschelte sie sich auf eine der holz-geschnitzten Bänke, die in den Erkern standen und betrach-tete die reichbestickten Fahnen, die darauf warteten, wieder geschwungen zu werden.

Die niedergehende Sonne tauchte den Raum in ein rötliches Licht, und es schien der Prinzessin, als würde sogar das Kaminfeuer zu flackern beginnen.

Eine behagliche Wärme begann den Saal zu durch-fluten, und während sie schlaftrunken auf die dunklen,

En pensant à tout cela, la princesse ne pouvait s'empêcher de rire. Ensuite elle montait en courant l'escalier étroit qui menait à la salle de banquet. Elle se blottissait contre une banquette de bois sculpté et passait en revue les bannières richement brodées qui attendaient de pouvoir flotter à nouveau.

Le soleil couchant baignait la pièce d'une lumière rougeâtre, et il semblait à la princesse que les bûches de l'âtre allaient se mettre à crépiter.

Une douce chaleur commençait à animer la salle, et tandis qu'elle fixait, songeuse, les sombres et vénérables

Frente a este idea, la princesa se echó a reír. Luego, subió corriendo por la escalera estrecha que conducía a la sala de banquetes. Se arrellanó en una banqueta de madera esculpida en uno de los miradores, y examinó los pendones de rico tejido que aguardaban ondear de nuevo.

El sol poniente inundaba la pieza con una luz rojiza y hasta le pareció a la princesa que la chimenea abierta se pondría a chisporrotear.

Un calor agradable iba animando la sala, y como la princesa miraba con fijeza, soñadora, a los cuadros som-

knights and chatelaines they portrayed climbed down from them and formed a truly regal train. One of them offered an arm to the princess, and she strode along with dignity to the evening's feast. Uniformed pages brought a never-ending succession of sumptuous dishes to the table, and the ruby red wine made the rounds.

How long the meal lasted she could not say. But her father's voice caused her to sit up.

"Princess, I have been looking for you everywhere. We were worried," he scolded. Though at the same time

✤✤✤✤✤✤✤✤✤✤✤✤✤✤✤✤✤✤✤✤✤✤

ehrwürdigen Gemälde starrte, begannen sich diese zu beleben; die Ritter und Burgfrauen stiegen herab und formten einen wahrhaft fürstlichen Zug. Sie reichten der Prinzessin den Arm und geleiteten sie würdevoll zum abendlichen Fest. Die Pagen brachten in endloser Folge köstliche Speisen zu Tisch, und der rote Wein machte die Runde.

Wie lange das Mahl dauerte, vermochte sie nicht zu sagen. Die Stimme des Vaters aber liess sie auffahren.

"Prinzessin, ich habe dich überall gesucht. Wir waren in Sorge um dich", schalt er. Doch gleichzeitig drückte er

tableaux, les chevaliers et les châtelaines en descendaient et formàient un cortège tout à fait princier. L'un d'eux offrait le bras à la princesse qui se dirigeait avec dignité vers le festin de la soirée. Des pages en uniforme apportaient une succession continue des plats, et le vin rouge rubis circulait autour de la table.

Elle ne saurait dire combien de temps dura le repas. Mais la voix de son père la fit se redresser.

«Princesse, je t'ai cherchée partout. Nous étions inquiets!» gronda-t-il. En même temps, il la serrait affec-

bríos y venerables, los caballeros y las castellanas bajaron de ellos y formaron una comitiva verdaderamente principesca. Le ofrecieron un brazo a la princesa y se dirigieron con dignidad hacia el festín de la tarde. Los pajes trajeron una sucesión continua de platos y el vino tinto circuló por la mesa.

No podría decir cuánto tiempo duró la cena. De repente, al oír la voz de su padre, se incorporó.

—Princesa, te busqué por todas partes. Estábamos preocupados por ti —la regañó su padre. Pero al mismo

his arms went around her lovingly and she felt safe and secure.

Then together they looked out the window and over the valley, over the rooftops of the village into the distant mists.

"Where does the fog come from?" the princess wanted to know.

"It comes from the waves that pound on the shore far, far away from here," her father said.

"And what lies beneath the fog?" she asked as she had many times before.

❧❧❧❧❧❧❧❧❧❧❧❧❧❧❧❧❧❧❧❧❧❧

sie so fest an sich, dass sie seine ganze Fürsorge spürte und sich geborgen fühlte.

Gemeinsam blickten sie dann aus dem Fenster über das Tal, über die Dächer des Dorfes hinweg, in die nebelverhangene Ferne.

"Woher kommt der Nebel?" wollte die Prinzessin wissen.

"Der kommt vom Wasser, das weit, weit fort von hier ans Ufer stösst", erklärte der Vater.

"Und was verbirgt der Nebel?" wollte sie weiter wissen.

tueusement dans ses bras, et elle se sentit tranquille et en sécurité.

Ensemble ils regardèrent par la fenêtre, au-delà de la vallée, au-delà des toits du village, vers la brume lointaine.

«D'où vient le brouillard?» voulait savoir la princesse.

«Il vient des vagues qui fouettent la rivage, loin, bien loin d'ici» repondit son père.

«Et qu'y-a-t-il sous le brouillard?» voulut-elle savoir encore.

tiempo la abrazaba fuerte, con todo su cariño, y ella se sintió tranquila y segura.

Luego, ambos miraron por la ventana, allende el valle, allende los tejados del pueblo, hacia la bruma lejana.

—?De dónde viene la niebla? —quiso saber la princesa.

—Viene del agua que golpea la costa, muy lejos de aquí —contestó su padre.

—?Y qué hay debajo de la niebla? —también quiso saber ella.

"The great city, where thousands and thousands of people live," he told her.

"Let me stay just a little longer," begged the princess. Inside, she felt the unaccountable longing to see the great city, and the distant waters seemed to beckon to her with an almost magnetic force.

Once alone again, the princess dropped down on her bench. Closing her eyes, she suddenly heard the musicians playing an enticement to dance. The colorful train of merry guests followed the standard bearer down into the courtyard. But the princess broke away from the procession...

⚜⚜⚜⚜⚜⚜⚜⚜⚜⚜⚜⚜⚜⚜⚜⚜⚜⚜⚜⚜⚜

"Er verbirgt die grosse Stadt, in der tausend und abertausend Menschen leben", erwiderte er.

"Lass mich noch für eine Weile hier sitzen", bat die Prinzessin. In ihrem Inneren fühlte sie eine unerklärliche Sehnsucht nach der grossen Stadt aufsteigen, und das ferne Wasser schien sie mit magnetischer Kraft anzuziehen.

Wieder allein, liess die Prinzessin sich auf ihrer Bank nieder. Sie schloss die Augen und hörte plötzlich das Spiel der Musikanten, das zum Tanz verlockte. Der bunte Zug der fröhlichen Gäste folgte den Fahnenträgern in den Hof hinab. Die Prinzessin aber löste sich aus der Reihe....

«La grande cité, où vivent des milliers et des milliers de gens» répondit-il.

«Laisse-moi rester encore un peu!» supplia la princesse. Elle était agitée par un désir inexplicable de voir la grande cité, et les vagues lointaines semblaient l'attirer avec une force presque magnétique.

De nouveau seule, elle se laissa retomber sur sa banquette. Elle ferma les yeux et écouta les musiciens jouer une invitation à la danse. Le cortège coloré et joyeux descendit dans la cour en suivant le porte-étendard. Mais là, la princesse se sépara du défilé....

❧❧❧❧❧❧❧❧❧❧❧❧❧❧❧❧❧❧❧❧❧

—La gran ciudad, en donde viven millares y millares de personas —respondió él.

—Déjame quedarme un poquito más —rogó la princesa. La agitaba un deseo inexplicable de ver a la gran ciudad, y el agua distante parecía atraerla con una fuerza magnética.

De nuevo a solas, se dejó caer en su banqueta. Cerró los ojos y escuchó a los músicos que tocaban, incitándola a bailar. El cortejo brillante de huéspedes alegres siguió al portador de estandarte que bajaba al patio. Pero la princesa se separó de la procesión. . .

She slipped past the grooms attending the horses, swung herself up onto the back of the finest black stallion and bolted out through the open castle gates. She raced along the dusty country road and past the village, never stopping, until she could no longer see the castle. Then she followed the course of a broad river, crossed a bridge and finally spotted the lights of the city in the distance.

Her cheeks were burning with excitement as she plunged ahead toward the lure of the city. The bustling streets there, she found, were washed with bright lights, and throngs of people were hurrying this way and that.

❖❖❖❖❖❖❖❖❖❖❖❖❖❖❖❖❖❖❖❖❖❖

Sie lief an den Knechten vorbei, welche die Pferde striegelten, schwang sich auf den Rücken des kräftigsten Rappen und trabte zum offenen Burgtor hinaus. Sie jagte die staubige Landstrasse entlang, vorbei am Dorf, ohne anzuhalten, bis sie die Burg nicht mehr sehen konnte. Sie folgte dem Lauf des mächtigen Stromes, überquerte eine Brücke und erblickte in der Ferne endlich die Lichter der Stadt.

Ihre Wangen glühten vor Aufregung, als sie sich in das verheissungsvolle Getümmel der Stadt stürzte. Die Strassen waren erfüllt von dem gleissenden Licht der Auslagen und Leuchtschilder, und ein Strom von Menschen eilte in diese und jene Richtung.

Elle se faufila derrière les valets qui prenaient soin des chevaux, enfourcha le meilleur étalon noir et fila à toute allure par les portes ouvertes du château. Elle galopa le long de la route de campagne poussiéreuse et dépassa le village sans s'arrêter, jusqu'à ce qu'elle ne vît plus le château. Elle suivit la berge d'une large rivière, franchit un pont et aperçut au loin les lumières de la ville.

Ses pommettes brûlaient d'excitation comme elle se précipitait vers l'appât de la cité. Les rues animées étaient baignées de lumières brillantes et des foules de gens se hâtaient dans tous les sens.

❖❖❖❖❖❖❖❖❖❖❖❖❖❖❖❖❖❖❖❖❖❖

Se coló entre los mozos de cuadra, se lanzó sobre el mejor caballo negro y pasó volando por las puertas abiertas del castillo. Corrió a lo largo de la carretera rural polvorienta y dejó el pueblo atrás, sin pararse, hasta que ya no pudo ver el castillo. Siguió la orilla de un río ancho, cruzó un puente y por fin, divisó a lo lejos las luces de la ciudad.

Al hundirse en el bullicio de la ciudad le ardían las mejillas de excitación. Luces brillantes inundaban las calles y riadas de gente se apresuraban en todas las direcciones.

The princess gazed up in awe as she approached the cathedral. What splendor, she thought, compared to the modest village church at home. She continued on, staring wide-eyed at the majestic palaces along the avenues, the magnificently-sculpted fountains, the parks bursting with colorful blossoms. People passed her, young and old, cheerful and scowling, yet no one noticed her, no one paid her any attention.

Suddenly she felt very lonely. I wish my father were here, she thought. I would enjoy the city twice as much if he were with me. "Shared happiness is doubled joy," it occured to her.

✤✤✤✤✤✤✤✤✤✤✤✤✤✤✤✤✤✤✤✤✤✤

Staunend blieb die Prinzessin vor der Kathedrale stehen. Was für ein Prunk war das doch im Vergleich zu der bescheidenen Dorfkirche daheim, dachte sie. Sie bestaunte die Paläste entlang der breiten Alleen, die prachtvollen Brunnen mit ihren Wasserspielen und die Parkanlagen mit der Überfülle ihrer Blumenpracht. Menschen gingen an ihr vorbei, junge und alte, heitere und ernste, doch niemand beachtete sie, niemand nahm sie wahr.

Sie fühlte sich mit einem Mal sehr einsam und dachte: "Ich wünschte, der Vater wäre hier. Die Stadt würde mir dann zweimal so gut gefallen. Geteilte Freude ist doppelte Freude", fuhr es ihr durch den Kopf.

La princesse leva un regard émerveillé en arrivant à la cathédrale. Quelle splendeur, pensa-t-elle, à côtè de la modeste église du village. Elle avançait, les yeux écarquillés, regardant les palaces longeant les avenues, les fontaines magnifiquement sculptées, les parcs à la floraison exubérante. Des gens la dépassaient, jeunes et vieux, gais et graves, mais pourtant personne ne la remarquait, personne ne faisait attention à elle.

Soudain, elle se sentit très seule. «J'aimerais que mon père soit là» pensa-t-elle. «La ville me plairait deux fois plus s'il était avec moi. Le bonheur partagé est une double joie» se dit-elle.

✠✠✠✠✠✠✠✠✠✠✠✠✠✠✠✠✠✠✠✠✠✠✠✠

La princesa se detuvo, asombrada, enfrente de la catedral. ¡Qué esplendor!, comparada con la modesta iglesia de su aldea, pensó. Atisbaba, maravillada, los palacios que bordeaban les avenidas, las fuentes magníficas con sus surtidores, los parques con su exuberancia floral. La gente pasaba delante de ella, joven y vieja, alegre y grave, sin embargo nadie reparaba en ella, nadie le hacía caso.

Entonces, se sintió muy sola y murmuró: —!Ojaló estuviera mi padre acquí! La ciudad me gustaría aún más. Felicidad compartida es doble alegría —pensó.

She grabbed up the reins and rode on. The horse moved at a lively clip, carrying her along like the wind. As the noises of the city faded behind her, broad green meadows began to open up. The horse leaped over streams and hedgerows, ditches and boulders. Seagulls flew into view, accompanying them on their brisk ride, and all of a sudden the endless expanse of ocean was spreading out before her, far as the eye could see.

The waves lashed the rocky shore with thunderous gusts, then pulled back swiftly, gathering new force to pound the coast again.

❦❦❦❦❦❦❦❦❦❦❦❦❦❦❦❦❦❦❦❦❦❦

Sie schwang sich wieder auf ihr Pferd, ergriff die Zügel und ritt weiter. Mit Windeseile wurde sie davongetragen. Der Lärm der Stadt verebbte, und weite, grüne Wiesen begannen sich vor ihr zu erstrecken. Das Pferd sprang über Bäche und Hecken, über Gräben und Gestein. Möwen begannen durch die Luft zu segeln und ihren eiligen Ritt zu begleiten, und ganz unerwartet erstreckte sich plötzlich vor ihr die unendliche Weite des Meeres.

Peitschend klatschten die Wellen an das steinige Ufer, sie flossen zurück, nur um mit neuer Wucht an die Küste zu prallen.

Elle saisit les rênes et se mit en route. Le cheval allait comme un bolide, l'emportant comme le vent. Les bruits de la cité disparaissaient et de grandes prairies vertes s'étalaient devant elle. Le cheval sautait au-dessus des ruisseaux et des haies, des fossés et des rochers. Des mouettes apparurent, accompagnant leur course débridée, et soudain la princesse découvrit l'étendue infinie de l'océan qui s'étalait devant elle, à perte de vue.

Les vagues fouettaient la rive rocheuse de leur claquement puissant, puis refluaient, rassemblant une nouvelle force pour battre à nouveau la côte.

⚜⚜⚜⚜⚜⚜⚜⚜⚜⚜⚜⚜⚜⚜⚜⚜⚜⚜⚜⚜⚜

Montó en su caballo y se lanzó adelante, como arrastrada por el viento. Los ruidos de la ciudad desaparecían y se abrían grandes praderas verdes. El caballo saltaba por arroyos y encima de setos, peñas y zanjas. Algunas gaviotas comenzaron a acompañarlos en su carrera desenfrenada, y de repente la princesa descubrió la superficie infinita del oceano que se extendía ante ella.

Las olas azotaban la ribera peñascosa con fuertes golpeos, y refluían, reuniendo bastante fuerza para batir de nuevo la costa.

The princess was so overwhelmed by the sight of the rushing breakers that she forgot for a moment to climb down from her horse. But as her amazement subsided, she jumped down, threw off her shoes and began to climb barefoot from one rock to another. The water sprayed her legs as she moved nimbly to try and dodge the waves. Finally she settled herself on a huge boulder and listened to the melody of the sea.

She felt strangely moved by the boundless blue-green expanse surrounding her. Then she suddenly grew very lonely. If only my mother were here, she thought. I would

⚜⚜⚜⚜⚜⚜⚜⚜⚜⚜⚜⚜⚜⚜⚜⚜⚜⚜⚜⚜⚜⚜

Die Prinzessin war von dem Anblick des heranrollenden Wassers so überwältigt, dass sie vorerst vergass, vom Pferd abzusteigen. Als sie sich dann gefasst hatte, sprang sie herunter, warf ihre Schuhe fort und kletterte barfuss von einem Felsblock zum anderen. Das Wasser bespritzte ihre Beine, und sie versuchte, den Wellen davonzuhüpfen. Schliesslich liess sie sich auf einem Felsen nieder und lauschte der Melodie des Meeres.

Die grenzenlose Weite, die sie umgab, beunruhigte sie. Sie fühlte sich mit einem Mal sehr einsam und dachte: "Könnte doch die Mutter jetzt hier bei mir sein. Das Meer

La princesse était tellement saisie par le déferlement des vagues qu'elle en oublia un instant de descendre de cheval. Mais son étonnement s'estompa, elle sauta à terre, se déchaussa et grimpa pieds nus d'un rocher à l'autre. L'eau aspergeait ses jambes lorsqu'elle tentait d'éviter les vagues. Enfin, elle s'installa sur un gros rocher et écouta la mélodie de la mer.

Elle se sentait étrangement émue par la vaste étendue d'eau bleu-vert qui l'entourait. Elle se sentit soudain très seule. «Si seulement ma mère était là, avec moi. J'aimerais

⚜⚜⚜⚜⚜⚜⚜⚜⚜⚜⚜⚜⚜⚜⚜⚜⚜⚜⚜⚜⚜⚜

La princesa estaba tan asombrada al ver las oleadas, que olvidó por un instante apearse del caballo. Luego, saltó, se quitó los zapatos y trepó descalza de una peña a otra. El agua le rociaba las piernas mientras trataba de evitar las olas. Finalmente, se instaló sobre una peña grande y escuchó la melodía del mar.

La conmovía de manera extraña la extensión sin límites que la rodeaba. Se sintió sola y pensó:

—¡Ojalá estuviera mi madre aquí conmigo! Me gus-

love the sea twice as much if she were with me. "Shared happiness is doubled joy," echoed through her mind again. Quietly, she scanned the horizon, wondering what lay beyond the endless waters.

How long she may have sat there, staring out, she could not say. But suddenly she spotted a huge, silvery fish swimming along nearby. Quickly she eased into the water and jumped upon its back.

"Take me across the ocean," she implored. "I have to know what lies on the other side."

The fish lowered its head into the water and began to

❦❦❦❦❦❦❦❦❦❦❦❦❦❦❦❦❦❦❦❦❦

würde mir dann zweimal so gut gefallen. Geteilte Freude ist doppelte Freude," fuhr es ihr wieder durch den Sinn. Ruhig wanderten ihre Augen über den Horizont und suchten zu ergründen, was jenseits des Meeres lag.

Wie lange sie so dagesessen sein mochte, konnte sie nicht sagen. Plötzlich jedoch entdeckte sie einen grossen, silbrigen Fisch, der die Küste entlangschwamm. Schnell watete sie ins Wasser und schwang sich auf seinen Rücken.

"Bring mich über das Meer", bat sie den Fisch. "Ich muss wissen, was am anderen Ufer liegt."

Der Fisch tauchte mit dem Kopf unter und begann die

la mer deux fois plus en sa compagnie. Le bonheur partagé est une double joie», lui revint à l'esprit. En silence, elle scrutait l'horizon, se demandant ce qui se trouvait au-delà de l'interminable étendue d'eau.

Elle n'aurait su dire combien de temps elle resta assise à cet endroit. Mais soudain, elle aperçut un gros poisson argenté qui nageait près de la côté. Elle s'avança rapidement dans l'eau et sauta sur son dos.

«Fais-moi traverser la mer» implora-t-elle. «Il faut que je sache ce qui se trouve de l'autre côté.»

Le poisson plongea la tête dans l'eau et emporta la

❧❧❧❧❧❧❧❧❧❧❧❧❧❧❧❧❧❧❧❧❧❧

taría aún más el mar. Felicidad compartida es doble alegría —le vino a la mente. Sus ojos otearon el horizonte, intentando adivinar lo que había más allá del mar.

No podría decir cuanto tiempo se quedó allí sentada. Pero de pronto, vio un pez grande que nadaba a lo largo de la costa. Se adelantó en el agua y montó sobre su lomo.

—Hazme cruzar el mar —le dijo al pez—. Debo saber lo que hay al otro lado.

El pez metió la cabeza en el agua y fue transportando a

carry the princess across the waves. They continued on all day and into the night. At dawn, the princess saw the sun burst from the sea like a fiery golden explosion; at sunset, she watched as it sank into the waves like a glowing orange ball. She rode past wondrous islands whose white, sandy beaches were gently caressed by the waves. She even skirted coral reefs and found herself surrounded by the most colorful shoals of fish.

As much as seeing this delighted her, the fish said not a word, and the princess grew very lonely. If I could share this sight with my friends, she thought, I would adore it

❧❧❧❧❧❧❧❧❧❧❧❧❧❧❧❧❧❧❧❧❧

Prinzessin über die Wellen zu tragen. Sie schwammen den ganzen Tag bis in die Nacht hinein. Am Morgen sah die Prinzessin die Sonne wie eine feurige Explosion aus dem Meer hervorbrechen; am Abend schaute sie zu, wie die Sonne als glühender Ball in den Wellen versank. Sie kam vorbei an wundersamen Inseln, deren weisser Sandstrand vom Meer gestreichelt wurde. Sie schwamm an Korallenriffen vorbei und fand sich umringt von bunten Schwärmen der verschiedensten Fische.

So sehr ihr auch dieser Anblick gefiel, die Fische blieben stumm, und die Prinzessin wurde sehr einsam. "Könnte ich euren Anblick doch nur mit meinen Freundinnen teilen, ihr würdet mir zweimal so gut gefallen",

princess sur les ondes. Ils nagèrent toute la journée jusqu'
à la nuit. A l'aube, elle vit le soleil jaillir de la mer, en
une explosion de feu doré, au crépuscule elle le vit s'abîmer
dans les ondes comme un ballon orange incandescent. Elle
longea des îles merveilleuses aux plages de sable blanc
caressées par les vagues. Elle nagea près de récifs de corail
et se trouva entourée de bancs de poissons multicolores.

Bien que ce spectacle l'enchantât, elle se sentait très
seule car les poissons ne disaient pas un mot. «Si mes amis
pouvaient vous voir, je vous aimerais deux fois plus»

❧❧❧❧❧❧❧❧❧❧❧❧❧❧❧❧❧❧❧❧❧❧

la princesa por las ondas. Nadaron todo el día hasta la
noche. Por la mañana, veía ella el sol surgir del mar como
una explosión de fuego; por la tarde lo veía hundirse en el
mar como un globo rojeante. Pasó cerca de islas mara-
villosas con playas de arena blanca acariciadas por las
ondas. Nadó a lo largo de arrecifes de coral y se encontró
rodeada de bancos de peces multicolores.

Por más que le encantaba este espectáculo, los peces
no decían una palabra y ella se sintió sola.

—¡Ojalá pudiera compartir este espectáculo con mis
amigos! Me gustaría todo lo que me rodea aún más

181

twice as much. Shared happiness is double joy. These experiences are too wonderful for just one person, she realized. It is like having a great feast and no one to savor it with. Almost apologetically she called out, "Swim on, great fish—take me to the other shore! All of this beauty is too much for me alone."

Again a great longing rose within her. Yet she knew it was not for the great city that lay beyond the sea, but for the people who cared about her and in whose lives she mattered.

❧❧❧❧❧❧❧❧❧❧❧❧❧❧❧❧❧❧❧❧❧❧

klagte sie. "Geteilte Freude ist doppelte Freude", dachte sie. "All diese Eindrücke sind für einen allein zu überwältigend." Es kam ihr vor, als feierte sie ein grosses Fest, ohne von Freunden umgeben zu sein. Fast entschuldigend befahl sie: "Schwimm weiter, grosser Fisch—bring mich ans andere Ufer. Ich kann soviel Schönheit allein nicht ertragen."

Wieder stieg grosse Sehnsucht in ihr auf. Doch sie wusste, dass es diesmal nicht das Verlangen nach der grossen Stadt jenseits des Meeres war, sondern nach den Menschen, die sich um sie sorgten, in deren Leben sie eine Rolle spielte.

pensa-t-elle. Le bonheur partagé est une double joie. Ce spectacle est trop merveilleux pour une seule personne, se dit-elle. C'est comme si l'on avait un grand festin et personne pour le partager. En s'excusant presque, elle s'écria: «Nage, grand poisson, ramène-moi sur l'autre rive! Toute cette beauté, c'est trop pour moi toute seule!»

Une grande nostalgie l'envahit à nouveau. Pourtant elle savait que ce n'était pas par désir de voir la grande ville au-delà de la mer, mais de retrouver les gens qui la chérissaient et pour qui elle comptait.

✤✤✤✤✤✤✤✤✤✤✤✤✤✤✤✤✤✤✤✤✤✤✤

—lamentó—. Felicidad compartida es doble alegría. Este espectáculo es demasiado maravilloso para una sola. Es como si yo tuviera un gran festín y nadie con quien compartirlo—. Suplicó casi disculpándose:

—¡Nada, pez grande, llévame a la otra ribera! Es demasiada belleza para mí sola.

Otra vez la sumergía una gran nostalgia. Pero sabía que no era por la gran ciudad al otro lado del mar, sino por las personas que la querían y para quienes contaba.

Just then a feeling of fear gripped her. Was she still important to them? And were they worrying about her? All at once she wanted to get home as quickly as possible.

"Turn back," she called out to the fish. "I must return home. Hurry!"

When they finally approached the shore, the princess slid down from the fish's back and then strode through the water until she reached solid ground. She looked around for the horse, but it was nowhere in sight. All she could see was a huge, old land turtle lumbering along.

❖❖❖❖❖❖❖❖❖❖❖❖❖❖❖❖❖❖❖❖❖❖❖

Eine ungeheure Angst ergriff sie. War sie den Leuten daheim immer noch wichtig? Machten sie sich um ihretwillen Sorge? Sie wollte auf einmal so schnell wie möglich nach Hause gelangen.

"Kehr um", rief sie dem Fisch zu. "Ich möchte nach Hause. Beeil dich!"

Als sie endlich in die Nähe des Ufers gelangte, glitt sie vom Rücken des Fisches und lief mit langen Sätzen ans Land. Sie suchte nach ihrem Pferd, doch war es nirgends zu sehen. Sie fand nur eine grosse, alte Schildkröte, die bedächtig des Weges kroch.

Elle ressentit l'étreinte d'une forte crainte. Comptait-elle encore pour les siens? S'inquiétaient-ils à son sujet? Tout à coup, elle voulut rentrer à la maison le plus vite possible.

«Rebrousse chemin», dit-elle au poisson. «Il faut que je rentre à la maison. Dépêche-toi!»

Lorsqu'elle atteignit enfin le rivage, elle se laissa glisser du poisson et regagna la terre à grand pas. Elle chercha le cheval, mais ne le vit nulle part. Elle ne trouva qu'une grosse et vieille tortue qui avançait péniblement.

❖❖❖❖❖❖❖❖❖❖❖❖❖❖❖❖❖❖❖❖❖❖

Experimentaba un miedo tremendo. ¿Era ella importante todavía para los suyos? Seguían preocupándose por ella? Súbitamente quiso volver a casa tan pronto como fuera posible. —Date prisa, —dijo al pez—, tengo que volver cuanto antes.

Cuando por fin alcanzó la ribera, bajó del lomo del pez y a zancadas llegó a la tierra. Buscó el caballo pero sólo pudo encontrar una tortuga grande y vieja que avanzaba trabajosamente.

"Take me home as quickly as you can!" implored the princess, crawling up upon his broad back.

Obligingly, the turtle pulled in his head and plodded slowly forward, step by step. At times when the princess could no longer contain her impatience, she would slide down from his rounded shell and run ahead in long bounds.

But when, from sheer exhaustion, she finally had to stop and rest, the turtle would catch up with her and the princess would ruefully climb back up onto her steady companion's back.

⚜⚜⚜⚜⚜⚜⚜⚜⚜⚜⚜⚜⚜⚜⚜⚜⚜⚜⚜⚜

"Bring mich heim, so schnell du kannst!" flehte die Prinzessin sie an und kroch auf deren breiten Rücken.

Die Schildkröte aber zog den Kopf ein und kroch langsam weiter, Schritt für Schritt. Von Zeit zu Zeit, wenn die Prinzessin ihre Ungeduld nicht mehr bezähmen konnte, glitt sie herab von dem gekrümmten Schild und lief in langen Sprüngen voraus.

Doch wenn sie dann vor Erschöpfung am Wegrand rasten musste, holte die Schildkröte sie immer wieder ein, und reumütig kletterte die Prinzessin wieder zurück auf den Rücken ihres beständigen Begleiters.

«Emmène-moi à la maison aussi vite que tu pourras»,
implora la princesse, et elle grimpa sur son large dos.

La tortue étira obligeamment la tête et s'ébranla lentement, pas à pas. Quand la princesse ne pouvait plus con-
tenir davantage son impatience, elle glissait le long de la
carapace ronde et courait à toutes jambes.

Mais quand elle finissait par devoir s'arrêter de pur
épuisement sur le bord de la route, la tortue la rattrapait et,
à regret, la princesse grimpait à nouveau sur le dos de sa
solide compagne.

❧❧❧❧❧❧❧❧❧❧❧❧❧❧❧❧❧❧❧❧❧❧❧

—Llévame a casa tan pronto como puedas —imploró
la princesa y se subió a su concha.

Complaciente, la tortuga estiró la cabeza y avanzó lentamente, paso a paso. Cuando la princesa ya no podía con-
tener su impacienca, se bajaba de la concha redonda e iba
corriendo adelante.

Pero cuando finalmente, tenía que pararse de pura
extenuación al lado de la carretera, la tortuga la alcanzaba
y la princesa se subía de nuevo, con pesar, sobre el lomo de
su sólida compañera.

Never before had days, hours, even minutes seemed so agonizingly long to the princess. Her restlessness grew with every laborious step, every bend in the road.

Would they still recognize her after so long a time? Would her parents be well, and her friends? She was filled with uncertainty. From time to time, she peered ahead, hoping to catch a glimpse of the castle. Finally, far in the distance, she spotted it.

Now, she was running frantically up the hill, up the steps, through the halls, breathless, bathed in sweat.

❖❖❖❖❖❖❖❖❖❖❖❖❖❖❖❖❖❖❖❖❖❖❖❖

Noch nie zuvor waren ihr Tage, Stunden oder Minuten so unendlich lang erschienen. Mit jedem Schritt, mit jeder Biegung wuchs ihre Unrast.

Würde man sie daheim noch erkennen nach so langer Zeit? Würden die Eltern, die Freunde wohlauf sein? Angst schnürte ihr die Kehle zu. Sie reckte sich hoch auf, um Ausschau zu halten. Endlich, ganz in der Ferne, erblickte sie die Burg.

Nun lief sie in wilder Jagd den Berg hinauf, die Stiegen, die Gänge entlang, atemlos, schweissgebadet...

Jamais auparavant les jours, les heures et les minutes ne lui avaient paru si longs. Sa nervosité grandissait à chaque pas, à chaque tournant de la route.

Allaient-ils encore la reconnaître après si longtemps? Ses parents et ses amis, allaient-ils bien? Elle était remplie d'une grande incertitude. De temps en temps, elle scrutait le lointain en espérant apercevoir le château. Finalement, elle le distingua au loin.

Alors, elle courut à perdre haleine, jusqu-au sommet de la colline, en haut des marches, à travers les grandes salles, à bout de souffle, baignée de sueur.

❖❖❖❖❖❖❖❖❖❖❖❖❖❖❖❖❖❖❖❖❖

Nunca le habían parecido tan largos los días, las horas o los minutos. Su impaciencia crecía con cada paso, con cada curva de la carretera.

¿Iban a reconocerla después de tanto tiempo? ¿Estaban bien sus padres, sus amigos? La ahogaba el temor. Estiraba el cuello para columbrar el castillo. Por fin, lo divisó a lo lejos.

Entonces, se precipitó a todo correr hacia lo alto de la colina, de las escaleras, por las salas, sin aliento, bañada en sudor. . . . .

There stood her father. With care-worn eyes, he bent over his daughter and brushed back the wisps of hair from her forehead.

"Are you all right, Princess?" he asked, sounding almost apologetic for waking her.

"I came up to get you; they are waiting for you in the village. The dance there—it is about to start."

Without a word, the princess jumped up and hugged her father. Then she ran happily down the hill. Strictly speaking, she was not really a princess at all.

❧❧❧❧❧❧❧❧❧❧❧❧❧❧❧❧❧❧❧❧❧

Da stand ihr Vater. Besorgt beugte er sich über seine Tochter und strich ihr das Haar aus der Stirn.
"Fehlt dir etwas, Prinzessin?" fragte er fast entschuldigend, weil er sie geweckt hatte.

"Ich komme dich holen, denn man wartet im Dorf auf dich. Heute ist Tanzabend—es beginnt bald."

Wortlos sprang die Prinzessin auf und umarmte ihren Vater. Dann lief sie glücklich den Berg hinunter ins Dorf. Genaugenommen war sie gar keine Prinzessin.

Son père était là. Les yeux remplis d'inquiétude, il se pencha sur sa fille et repoussa les mèches folles de son front.

«Te sens-tu bien, Princesse?» demanda-t-il, s'excusant presque de l'avoir reveillée.

«Je suis monté te chercher; on t'attend au village. Il y a bal ce soir, il va commencer.»

Sans un mot, la princesse se leva d'un bond et étreignit son père. Puis, toute heureuse, elle descendit la colline en courant vers le village. A vrai dire, elle n'était pas du tout princesse.

⚜⚜⚜⚜⚜⚜⚜⚜⚜⚜⚜⚜⚜⚜⚜⚜⚜⚜⚜⚜⚜⚜

Allí estaba su padre. Con los ojos llenos de ternura, se inclinó hacia su hija y le apartó los cabellos de la frente.

—¿Te sientes bien, Princesa? —le preguntó solícitamente por haberla despertado—. Vine a buscarte; te están esperando en el pueblo. Hay un baile esta noche.

Sin una palabra, la princesa se enderezó y abrazó a su padre. Luego, feliz, corrió al pueblo. A decir verdad, no era realmente una princesa.

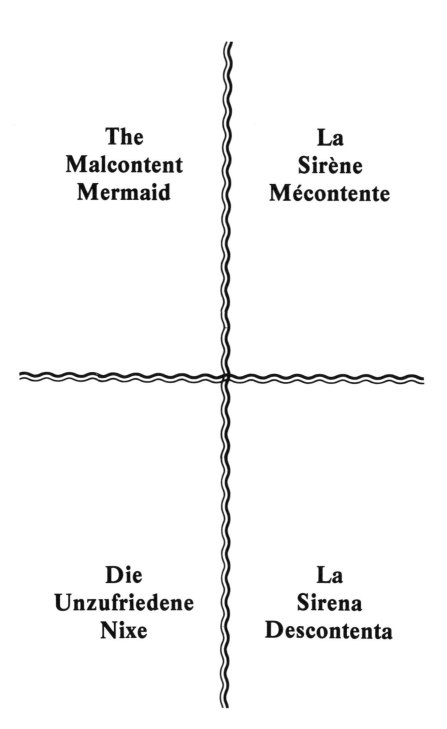

The
Malcontent
Mermaid

La
Sirène
Mécontente

Die
Unzufriedene
Nixe

La
Sirena
Descontenta

That year, there was as much overpopulation among the denizens of the deep as there was on earth. All the rivers and lakes were teeming with mermaids, and the mermen had to place their charges into swimming pools and park fountains so they would be kept moist.

This is how it happened that a graceful, young mermaid came to occupy the oval white pool soon after it was completed.

The pool was situated in the garden of a small, attractive home. Palm fronds were mirrored in the crystal-clear water, and on balmy evenings the heady scent of orange blossoms filled the air. Though the young mermaid had

Bei den Bewohnern der Gewässer war eine ebensolche Übervölkerung eingetreten wie oben auf der Erde. Alle Flüsse und Seen waren mit Nixen überfüllt, und die Wassermänner mussten ihre Schutzbefohlenen in Schwimmbecken und Brunnen unterbringen, um sie von Wasser benetzt zu halten.

So geschah es, dass eine zierliche, junge Nixe in das ovale, weisse Becken einzog, kaum dass es fertiggestellt worden war.

Das Schwimmbad lag im Garten eines kleinen, hübschen Hauses. Palmenblätter spiegelten sich im Wasser, und an warmen Abenden erfüllte der Duft der Orangenbäume die Luft. Die Nixe hätte allen Grund gehabt, mit

Cette année-là, la surpopulation atteignait les habitants des profondeurs autant que ceux de la terre. Toutes les rivières, tous les lacs grouillaient de sirènes, et les tritons devaient placer les jeunes sous leur garde dans les piscines et les fontaines des parcs pour leur assurer l'humidité nécessaire.

C'est ainsi qu'une jeune et gracieuse sirène vint à occuper la piscine blanche, de forme ovale, peu après la fin de sa construction.

Cette piscine se trouvait dans le jardin d'une jolie petite villa. Les feuilles des palmiers se reflétaient dans l'eau claire comme le cristal, et par les douces soirées, la senteur capiteuse des fleurs d'oranger emplissait l'air.

~~~~~~

Ese año, había tanto exceso de población entre los habitantes de las profundidades como lo había sobre La Tierra. Todos los ríos y lagos rebosaban de sirenas, y los tritones tenían que zambullirse en piscinas y fuentes de los parques para que no se les secara la piel.

Fue así como sucedió que una graciosa y joven sirena llegó a ocupar la oval piscina blanca en cuanto quedó terminada.

La piscina estaba situada en el jardín de una pequeña y atractiva casa. En el agua cristalina se reflejaban las hojas de palma y la embriagadora fragancia de los azahares saturaba el ambiente de los apacibles atarcederes. Aun-

every reason to be happy in her new home, still she thrust out her lower lip resentfully and submerged herself in the deepest point of the basin.

"What to you want of me?" asked the merman. "You have a splendid basin all your own. The other mermaids have to crowd together in aquariums with barely enough room to stretch out their fins."

"But they are able to play with the fish," the mermaid pouted. "They can race them or ride on them. They can play hide-and-seek among the plants or slip into the empty

ihrem neuen Heim zufrieden zu sein. Sie aber schob trotzig die Unterlippe vor und liess sich an der tiefsten Stelle des Bassins zu Boden sinken.

"Was willst du von mir?" fragte sie der Wassermann. "Du hast ein prachtvolles Becken ganz für dich allein. Andere Nixen müssen sich in Aquarien zusammendrängen und haben kaum Platz, um ihre Flossen auszustrecken."

"Aber dafür können sie mit den Fischen spielen", maulte die Nixe. "Sie können mit ihnen um die Wette schwimmen oder auf ihnen reiten. Sie können zwischen den Algen Verstecken spielen oder in leere Muscheln

Bien que la jeune sirène eût tout pour être heureuse dans sa nouvelle demeure, elle fit néanmoins une moue de dépit et s'enfonça dans le coin le plus profond du bassin.

«Que me veux-tu?» demanda le triton. «Tu as un bassin splendide pour toi toute seule. Les autres sirènes doivent s'entasser dans des aquariums avec à peine assez de place pour étaler leurs nageoires.»

«Mais elles peuvent jouer avec les poissons» dit la sirène en boudant. «Elles peuvent faire la course avec eux, ou monter sur leur dos. Elles peuvent jouer à cache-cache parmi les plantes, ou se glisser à l'intérieur des

que la joven sirena tenía muchas razones porque sentirse contenta en su nuevo hogar, fruncía su labio inferior en señal de resentimiento y se sumergía en el punto más profundo del estanque.

—¿Qué quieres de mí? —le preguntó el tritón—. Tienes un espléndido estanque todo para ti. Las otras sirenas viven apretadas en acuarios con un espacio apenas suficiente para estirar sus aletas.

—Pero pueden jugar con los peces —contestó la sirena refunfuñando.

—Pueden hacerlos competir en regatas o montarlos. Pueden jugar a las escondidas entre las plantas o meterse

shells," she said, "while I can't do anything but swim back and forth. It bores me to death," she lamented and glared reproachfully at the merman.

His surprise turned to anger.

"Your task is to keep watch so that no one meets with an accident in the water, but what are you thinking about? Only of your pleasure. You young ones nowadays have no sense of responsibility," he boomed. "All you care about is diversion and fun. We older ones have to do all the work

schlüpfen", meinte sie, "während ich hier nichts anderes machen kann, als hin und her schwimmen. Es ist zum Sterben langweilig", jammerte sie und sah den Wassermann vorwurfsvoll an.

Dessen Verwunderung schlug in Ärger um.

"Deine Aufgabe ist es aufzupassen, dass niemandem im Wasser ein Unglück zustösst! Doch woran denkst du? Nur an dein Vergnügen! Die Jugend heutzutage hat überhaupt kein Verantwortungsbewusstsein!" donnerte er. "Alles, was ihr sucht, ist Abwechslung und Vergnügen. Die Arbeit aber müssen wir Alten machen, während ihr herum-

coquillages vides, dit elle, tandis que moi, je ne peux faire rien d'autre que nager en rond. Je m'ennuie à mourir!» se lamentait-elle, en lançant au triton des regards chargés de reproche.

Sa surprise tourna à la colère.

«Ton devoir est de veiller à ce que personne n'ait d'accident dans l'eau, mais à quoi est-ce que tu penses? Uniquement à ton plaisir. Les jeunes d'aujourd'hui n'ont aucun sens des responsabilités» gronda-t-il. «Tout ce qui vous intéresse, c'est de vous distraire et de vous amuser. Nous, les anciens, nous devons faire tout le travail pendant

en conchas vacías —dijo ella—, mientras que yo no puedo hacer nada más que nadar de un lado al otro. Me aburre mucho —se lamentó mirando al tritón con reproche.

La sorpresa del tritón se convirtió en enojo.

—¿Tu tarea es vigilar que nadie tenga un accidente en el agua, sin embargo, en qué estás pensando? Sólo en tu placer. Los jóvenes no tienen ningún sentido de responsabilidad hoy en día —rugió él—. Lo único que les interesa es el entretenimiento y la diversión. Nosotros los mayores tenemos que hacer todo el trabajo mientras juegan y son

while you play around and are good for nothing." In his vexation, he reached out and shook the young mermaid so sharply that several of her shiny blue scales drifted to the bottom of the pool. Then he released her and disappeared.

Once alone again, the mermaid let her slender, graceful form glide silently through the water, only a hint of a wave betraying her presence.

Nobody noticed her. The man who came with a long-handled net to fish out the leaves from the bottom of the pool and who nearly caught her tail with it did not notice her. The woman who arrived to sunbathe on a yellow

spielt und zu nichts zu gebrauchen seid." In seinem Zorn ergriff er die Nixe und beutelte sie so heftig, dass ein paar ihrer blauschimmernden Schuppen abfielen und in die Tiefe sanken. Da liess er von ihr ab und verschwand.

Alleingelassen, liess die Nixe ihren schlanken Körper so sanft durch das Wasser gleiten, dass nur der Hauch eines Wellenschlages ihre Anwesenheit verriet.

Niemand nahm sie wahr. Der Mann, der mit einem langstieligen Netz die auf den Boden gesunkenen Blätter herausfischte und dabei um ein Haar ihre Schwanzflosse gefangen hätte, bemerkte sie nicht. Die Frau, die sich im Becken auf einer gelben Gummimatratze sonnte und laut

que vous vous amusez et vous n'êtes bons à rien!» Il était si irrité qu'il attrapa la jeune sirène et la secoua si fort que plusieurs de ses écailles bleues vernissées tombèrent au fond de la piscine. Puis il la relâcha et disparut.

De nouveau seule, la sirène laissa son corps mince et gracieux glisser silencieusement dans l'eau, seul un imperceptible sillage trahissant sa présence.

Personne ne la remarquait. Ni l'homme qui vint avec son filet à long manche pêcher les feuilles du fond de la piscine, et qui faillit attraper sa queue; ni la dame qui vint prendre un bain de soleil dans la piscine sur un matelas

unos buenos para nada.

En su vejación, agarró y sacudió a la joven sirena tan rudamente que varias de sus brillantes escamas azules cayeron al fondo de la piscina. Después la soltó y desapareció.

En cuanto se quedó sola de nuevo, la sirena dejó que su esbelta y graciosa figura se deslizara silenciosamente por el agua, con sólo la insinuación de una ola denunciando su presencia.

Nadie la advertía. El hombre que vino a sacar las hojas del fondo de la piscina con una red de mango largo y que casi atrapa su cola con ella, no la notó. La mujer que llegó para tomar un baño de sol sobre un flotador de goma

rubber float in the pool and who screamed when a sudden ripple made her suit wet did not notice her. Nor did the woman's baby, who crawled around the garden on all fours, and whose loud bawling unnerved the mermaid until at last his nanny came and carried him away.

Only the dog, an old, red-haired setter, came running and began to bark as the mermaid swam to and fro. Wagging his tail, he bent down, trying to touch her with his forepaw, and nearly fell into the water.

"What's the matter with that dog again today?" the woman wondered aloud. "He's so restless." Then she

aufschrie, wenn eine Welle ihren Badeanzug benetzte, bemerkte sie nicht. Und schon gar nicht das Baby, das auf allen Vieren im Garten herumkroch und mit seinem lauten Geplärr der Nixe so lange auf die Nerven ging, bis endlich das Kindermädchen aus dem Haus gelaufen kam und den Schreier davontrug.

Lediglich der Haushund, ein alter, rothaariger Setter, kam aufgeregt bellend angelaufen, während die Nixe hin und her schwamm. Er wedelte mit dem Schwanz, senkte den Kopf und versuchte, mit der Vorderpfote nach ihr zu greifen, wobei er fast selbst ins Wasser gefallen wäre.

"Was der Hund heute wieder hat?" wunderte sich die Frau. "Er ist so unruhig." Sie erhob sich von der Schwimm-

flottant jaune, et cria lorsqu'une ride sur l'eau, inattendue, mouilla son maillot de bain; ni le bébé de cette dame, qui rampait à quatre pattes dans le jardin et dont les cris aigus agacèrent la sirène jusqu'à ce que la gouvernante vienne le chercher.

Seul le chien, un vieux setter à poils roux, arriva en courant et se mit à aboyer pendant que la sirène nageait de-ci de-là. Il pencha la tête en remuant la queue et faillit tomber dans l'eau en essayant de la toucher avec sa patte.

«Qu'est-ce qu'il a encore ce chien, aujourd'hui?» dit la dame tout haut. «Il est si agité!» Puis elle se leva, abandon-

amarillo en la piscina y que gritó cuando una repentina onda mojó su traje, no la notó. Tampoco lo hizo el bebé de la mujer, quien gateó alrededor del jardín y cuyo fuerte llanto enervó a la sirena hasta cuando su niñera se lo llevó.

Solamente el perro, un viejo y pelirrojo Setter, se acercó corriendo y empezó a ladrar mientras la sirena nadaba de aquí para allá. Meneando su rabo, se agachó tratando de tocarla con su pata delantera, y casi se cae en el agua.

—¿Qué le pasa hoy otra vez a ese perro? —la mujer se preguntó en voz alta—. Está muy inquieto.

rose from the rubber float, tiptoed out of the pool and headed for the house.

At first, the mermaid found it quite entertaining to play with the dog. She teased him and enjoyed it when he growled and scampered after her.

But in time she grew tired of this and looked around for a new diversion. Then she spotted the long, black wrap-around robe the woman had left on one of the chairs. Was she coming back for it? The mermaid waited and watched. She liked the robe. And she would love to try on human's clothes.

matratze, stieg aus dem Bad und ging zum Haus.

Anfänglich fand die Nixe das Spiel mit dem Hund ganz unterhaltsam. Sie neckte ihn und freute sich, wenn er knurrend nach ihr schnappte.

Schliesslich aber wurde sie dessen überdrüssig und suchte nach einer neuen Abwechslung. Sie erblickte den langen, schwarzen Wickelrock, den die Frau über einen der Sessel gelegt hatte. Würde sie ihn holen kommen? Die Nixe wartete und blickte herum. Der Rock gefiel ihr. So gerne hätte sie einmal Menschenkleider anprobiert.

nant le matelas flottant, quitta la piscine sur la pointe des pieds et se dirigea vers la maison.

Tout d'abord, la sirène trouva très amusant de jouer avec le chien. Elle le taquinait et s'amusait à le voir grogner et folâtrer avec elle.

Mais au bout d'un moment elle s'en lassa et rechercha une nouvelle distraction. Elle aperçut alors le long peignoir portefeuille noir que la dame avait laissé sur une des chaises. Reviendrait-elle le chercher? La sirène attendit en regardant. Le peignoir lui plaisait. Elle brûlait d'essayer des vêtements d'êtres humains.

Enseguida se levantó del flotador de goma, salió de la piscina de puntillas y se dirigió hacia la casa.

Al principio, a la sirena le pareció entretenido jugar con el perro. Lo molestaba y se divertía cuando gruñía y corría tras ella.

Pero con el tiempo se cansó de eso y empezó a buscar una nueva diversión. Entonces localizó la larga y abrigadora bata negra que la mujer había colgado sobre una de las sillas. ¿Regresará por ella? La sirena observó y esperó. Le gustaba la bata y además, le encantaba la idea de ponerse ropa humana.

Moments passed, but the woman did not return. Did she dare to quickly slip on the robe? The mermaid continued to watch and wait. Finally, she quietly pulled herself from the water, flopped carefully toward the chair and grabbed up the robe. It took quite a while before she could figure out how to put it on. At last, she succeeded.

Now she paraded grandly before the large glass panel in the garden door, enchanted by her own appearance. She placed one hand on her hip and swayed from side to side. Then it dawned on her: in this robe, I could even go out among people. The mermaid looked longingly at the garden

Die Zeit verstrich, doch die Frau kam nicht zurück. Ob sie es wohl wagen konnte, den Rock schnell anzuziehen? Wieder lauschte und wartete sie. Schliesslich glitt sie aus dem Wasser, zappelte vorsichtig zu dem Sessel und ergriff den Rock. Es dauerte eine ganze Weile, bevor ihr klar wurde, wie der Rock anzuziehen war. Endlich aber gelang es ihr.

Nun paradierte sie vor der grossen Scheibe der Gartentür auf und ab und war ganz entzückt über ihre eigene Erscheinung. Sie stützte eine Hand in die Hüfte und wiegte sich hin und her. Dann überlegte sie: "In diesem Rock könnte ich sogar unter Menschen gehen." Sehnsüch-

Quelques minutes passèrent, la dame ne revenait pas. Oserait-elle enfiler rapidement le peignoir? La sirène continua d'attendre en guettant. Finalement, elle sortit doucement de l'eau, clopina prudemment vers la chaise et saisit le peignoir. Elle mit un certain temps à trouver comment le mettre. Elle y parvint enfin.

La voilà se pavanant fièrement devant la grande baie vitrée de la porte du jardin, ravie de son image. Elle se met une main sur la hanche et se dandine de droite à gauche. Alors elle se dit: avec ce peignoir de bain, je pourrais même sortir avec des êtres humains. La sirène regardait avec

Pasaron unos momentos, y la mujer no regresó. ¿Se atrevería a ponerse la bata rápidamente? La sirena continuó observando y esperando. Al fin, se salió del agua silenciosamente, aleteó cuidadosamente hacia la silla y cogió la bata. Le tomó un buen rato entender cómo ponérsela. Al fin, lo logró.

Ahora desfilaba pomposamente frente al largo panel de cristal de la puerta del jardín, encantada con su apariencia. Con una mano en la cadera, se meneó de lado a lado. Entonces se le ocurrió que en esta bata, podría incluso, andar entre la gente. La sirena miró ansiosamente hacia la

door. She would love to see what the outside world looked like. She turned and glanced at the house, listening for any sounds of stirring inside, but it remained quiet as before.

At last, the mermaid carefully draped the long robe over her tail, then slid toward the garden door and opened it cautiously. She stuck out her head, looking from side to side. Along the sunny street she saw a row of small, neat houses, surrounded by gardens in colorful bloom. It was so peaceful and quiet that she gained the courage to venture a few steps down the walk, then a few more. Suddenly, she felt so free and elated she almost cried out for joy.

tig blickte sie nach der Gartentür. Sie hätte so gerne einmal gesehen, wie die Welt ausserhalb des Gartens aussah. Sie blickte zum Haus und horchte, ob sich drinnen etwas rührte, doch es blieb so still wie zuvor.

Die Nixe legte nun mit grosser Sorgfalt den langen Rock über die Schwanzflosse, dann glitt sie zur Gartentür und öffnete sie vorsichtig. Sie steckte ihren Kopf hinaus und blickte nach beiden Seiten. Entlang der sonnigen Strasse erstreckte sich eine Reihe kleiner, hübscher Häuser, umgeben von bunt blühenden Gärten. Es war so ruhig und friedlich, dass sie ein paar Schritte hinaus wagte, und dann noch einige. Sie fühlte sich so frei und glücklich, dass sie am liebsten vor Freude gejubelt hätte.

envie la porte du jardin. Elle brûlait de voir à quoi ressemblait le monde au-dehors. Elle se retourna et jeta un coup d'œil vers la maison, tendant l'oreille pour déceler le moindre mouvement à l'intérieur, mais tout restait calme.

Finalement, la sirène drapa soigneusement sa queue dans le long peignoir, se glissa vers le portail du jardin et l'ouvrit prudemment. Elle sortit la tête à l'extérieur, regardant de droite à gauche. Elle vit, bordant la rue ensoleillée, une rangée de jolies petites maisons entourées de jardins en fleurs. Tout était si paisible et si tranquille qu'elle trouva le courage de s'aventurer sur le trottoir en faisant quelques pas, puis encore quelques autres. Tout à coup, elle se sentit si libre et si exaltée qu'elle pleura presque de joie.

puerta del jardín. Le encantaría conocer el mundo exterior. Se volteó y miró hacia la casa, tratando de escuchar cualquier sonido de movimiento que viniese de ella, pero seguía silenciosa como antes.

Finalmente, la sirena extendió la larga bata sobre su cola, después se deslizó hacia la puerta del jardín y la abrió cuidadosamente. Sacó su cabeza, mirando de lado a lado. A lo large de la calle soleada, vió una hilera de casas pequeñas y pulcras, rodeadas de jardines que florecían vistosamente. Estaba todo tan apacible y tranquilo que se hizo de valor para dar unos cuantos pasos en el camino, después unos cuantos más. Súbitamente, se sintió tan libre y jubilosa que casi lloraba de alegría.

At the end of the block she saw a small group of people standing around. She yearned to join them, talk with them, perhaps even make some friends. No longer was she willing to remain by herself, bored and lonely, at the bottom of the pool. She wanted to be free and now she knew she could be!

Spurred on by this realization, the mermaid started slowly down the sidewalk toward where the people were standing. The hard pavement scratched her fins, but at least knowing they were hidden from sight beneath the long robe comforted her.

Am Ende der Strasse sah sie eine kleine Gruppe von Leuten. Zu denen wollte sie gehen, mit ihnen sprechen, vielleicht sogar eine Freundschaft schliessen. Nur allein wollte sie nicht mehr bleiben, gelangweilt und einsam am Grund des Schwimmbeckens. Sie wollte frei sein und wusste nun, dass sie es auch sein konnte.

Von dieser Erkenntnis getrieben, begann die Nixe langsam den Gehsteig entlang zu gehen, den Leuten entgegen. Das harte Plaster zerkratzte ihre Flosse, doch zumindest das Bewusstsein, diese unter dem langen Rock verborgen zu haben, beruhigte sie.

Au bout de la rue, elle vit un petit groupe de gens. Elle mourait d'envie de les rejoindre, de leur parler, peut-être même de se faire des amis. Elle ne voulait plus rester seule, dans l'ennui et la solitude, au fond de la piscine. Elle désirait être libre et maintenant elle était sûre qu'elle pouvait l'être!

Aiguillonnée par cette révélation, la sirène avança lentement sur le trottoir vers l'endroit où les gens se trouvaient. Les durs pavés écorchaient ses nageoires, mais l'idée de savoir qu'elles étaient dissimulées par le long peignoir lui redonnait courage.

Al final de la calle, notó que había un pequeño grupo de gente. Anhelaba reunirse y hablar con ellos, e incluso tal vez hacer amistad. Ya no quería estar sola, aburrida y solitaria en el fondo de la piscina. ¡Quería ser libre y ahora sabía que podía serlo!

Impulsada por este pensamiento, la sirena se puso en marcha lentamente por la acera hacia donde estaba la gente. El pavimento rígido rasguñaba sus aletas, pero el saber que estaban ocultas bajo la larga bata le confortaba.

And as to why she shuffled a bit when she walked, should any of the people in the group ask her about it, she knew she could come up with some sort of explanation. Buoyed by this, she continued on down the block, but when she finally reached the cluster of people nobody asked her anything nor even returned her smile. In fact, the people were just standing around silently, simply staring into space.

What's wrong with them, the mermaid wondered. Aren't they happy to have met one another, to have so many people to talk with?

Und was den hinkenden Gang betraf, so würde sie schon eine Erklärung dafür finden, sollte jemand danach fragen. Ermutigt ging sie weiter, doch als sie endlich die Menschengruppe erreichte, da fragte niemand nach ihrem Gebrechen, noch erwiderte jemand ihr Lächeln. Die Leute standen vielmehr schweigend herum und starrten einfach ins Leere.

"Was ist denn mit denen los?" wunderte sich die Nixe. "Warum freuen sie sich nicht darüber, einander getroffen zu haben und miteinander reden zu können?"

Et pour ce qui était de sa démarche traînante, si quelqu'un lui en demandait la raison, elle pourrait toujours trouver une explication quelconque. Ainsi encouragée par cette idée, elle alla jusqu'au bout de la rue, mais lorsqu'elle arriva enfin près du petit attroupement, personne ne lui demanda quoi que ce soit, ni ne lui rendit son sourire. En fait, les gens se tenaient juste là, debout, en silence, le regard vague.

«Qu'est-ce qu'ils ont?» se demandait la sirène. «Ne sont-ils pas heureux de se rencontrer, d'avoir tant de gens avec qui parler?»

Y en cuanto a por qué se arrastraba un poco al caminar, si es que alguien del grupo se lo preguntara, ella sabría darles alguna explicación. Alentada por esto, continuó avanzando por la cuadra, pero cuando finalmente llegó a donde estaba el grupo de gente, nadie le preguntó nada y ni siquiera le devolvieron la sonrisa. Esas personas estaban paradas ahí en silencio, mirando fijamente hacia el vacío.

—¿Qué les pasa? —se preguntaba la sirena—. ¿Acaso no están felices de haberse conocido, de tener tanta gente con quien charlar?

She started to shake her head in dismay when suddenly she was jolted by the noisy rumble of a large bus, which rolled to a stop at the curb in front of her, its doors opening with a bang. As she looked on uncertainly, the people around her began to board the bus. She was the last one to hop up the steps.

The driver thrust out his hand. The mermaid looked at him, puzzled.

"You have to pay the fare," he said.

"But, I have no money," she replied. "And my feet hurt, I cannot walk very far..."

Bedauernd schüttelte sie den Kopf, doch wurde sie durch den Lärm eines heranbrausenden, grossen Autobusses aus ihren Überlegungen gerissen. Der Bus blieb am Strassenrand vor ihr stehen und klappte die Türen auf. Sie schaute unsicher um sich, während die Leute um sie herum den Bus bestiegen. Sie hüpfte als letzte die Stufen hinauf.

Der Fahrer hielt ihr die offene Hand entgegen. Die Nixe schaute ihn verständnislos an.

"Du musst das Fahrgeld zahlen", sagte er.

"Aber ich habe kein Geld", erwiderte sie. "Und meine Füsse schmerzen, ich kann nicht sehr weit gehen."

Elle hochait la tête avec consternation quand tout à coup, le vrombissement d'un gros bus la fit sursauter. Il s'arrêta juste devant elle, le long du trottoir, en ouvrant ses portes avec un bruit sec. Elle regardait, inquiète, tandis que les gens commençaient à monter dans le bus. Elle fut la dernière à sauter sur les marches.

Le chauffeur tendit la main vers elle. La sirène le regarda, déconcertée.

«Il faut payer le ticket» dit-il.

«Mais je n'ai pas d'argent» répondit-elle. «Et mes pieds me font mal, je ne peux pas marcher bien loin...»

Empezaba a menear la cabeza consternada cuando, repentinamente la sacudió el estrepitoso ruido de un autobús grande que avanzó hasta una parada situada en la acera frente a ella, abriendo sus puertas con gran alboroto. Mientras ella observaba con incertidumbre, la gente a su alrededor empezó a abordar el autobús. Ella fue la última en subir las escalerillas.

El conductor extendió la mano. La sirena le miró, perpleja.

—Tienes que pagar el pasaje —dijo el.

—Pero no tengo dinero —contestó ella—. Y me duelen los pies, no puedo caminar mucha distancia.

The driver shook his head.

"Without money, you cannot ride the bus." Adding, "Blisters, you can get free of charge." At these words, he pushed her down the steps, closed the door in her face and drove away.

While this was not what the mermaid had expected, she didn't grow discouraged easily. Instead, she trudged down the street and soon was surrounded by heavy traffic. Motorists honked at her, yelled at her, even whistled at her and she began to feel uneasy. But she pressed on, moving faster and faster despite the painful ache in her tail.

Der Fahrer schüttelte unerbittlich mit dem Kopf.

"Ohne Geld kannst du nicht mitfahren. Doch Blasen kannst du dir umsonst holen", fügte er hinzu. Mit diesen Worten drängte er sie die Stufen hinunter, klappte die Tür vor ihr zu und fuhr davon.

Das war nicht gerade, was die Nixe erhofft hatte, doch liess sie sich nicht so leicht entmutigen. Sie marschierte auf der Strasse weiter, wo sie bald dichter Verkehr umgab. Sie wurde angehupt, angeschrien, sogar angepfiffen und bekam richtiggehend Angst. Doch sie ging weiter, immer schneller, trotz der Schmerzen in ihrer Flosse.

Le chauffeur hocha la tête.

«Sans argent, vous ne pouvez pas prendre le bus.» Et il ajouta: «Mais les ampoules, elles, sont gratuites.» Ce disant, il la repoussa au bas des marches, lui ferma la porte au nez, et repartit.

Même si ce n'était pas ce à quoi la sirène s'attendait, elle ne se laissa pas décourager facilement. Alors, elle descendit péniblement la rue et se trouva vite en plein trafic. Les conducteurs klaxonnaient, criaient ou même sifflaient, et elle commença à se sentir mal à l'aise. Mais elle continua d'aller le plus vite possible, malgré la pénible douleur qu'elle ressentait dans sa queue.

El conductor meneó la cabeza. —Sin dinero no puedes viajar en el autobús —añadiendo—, las ampollas, esas las puedes obtener gratis.

Con estas palabras, la empujó escaleras abajo, cerró la puerta en su cara y se alejó a toda prisa.

Aunque esto no fue lo que la sirena esperaba, no se dejó desanimar fácilmente. Al contrario, recorrió la calle trabajosamente y pronto se encontró rodeada de un tráfico muy pesado. Los automovilistas le tocaban la bocina, le gritaban, incluso le silbaban, y ella empezó a sentirse inquieta. Sin embargo se apresuró, moviéndose más y más rápido a pesar del dolor en su cola.

Finally, she arrived at a large square. People were sitting around tree-shaded tables, talking and laughing. Under a huge umbrella, waiters standing behind a counter were dispensing cold drinks in tall, frosty glasses. Only now did the mermaid realize how tired and thirsty she was. She knew a sip of water would revive her. But when she made her way to the counter and asked for water, the waiter held out his hand.

"I have no money," she said. "All I want is a glass of water."

Endlich gelangte sie zu einem grossen Platz. Lachende Menschen sassen an Kaffeehaustischen im Schatten der Bäume und unterhielten sich. Unter einem riesigen Sonnenschirm standen Kellner hinter einer Theke und verteilten in hohen Gläsern eisgekühlte Getränke. Erst jetzt bemerkte die Nixe, wie erschöpft und durstig sie war. Ein Schluck Wasser würde sie beleben, dachte sie. Doch als sie an die Bar trat und um ein Glas Wasser bat, da hielt der Kellner die Hand auf.

"Ich habe kein Geld", sagte sie. "Alles was ich möchte, ist ein Glas Wasser."

Finalement, elle atteignit un grand square. Des gens, assis à des tables à l'ombre des arbres, parlaient et riaient. Sous un énorme parasol, des garçons de café distribuaient, de derrière leur comptoir, des rafraîchissements dans de grands verres givrés. C'est à ce moment là que la sirène se rendit compte combien elle était fatiguée et assoiffée. Elle était sûre qu'une gorgée d'eau lui redonnerait vie. Mais lorsqu'elle s'avança vers le comptoir pour demander de l'eau, le garçon de café tendit la main.

«Je n'ai pas d'argent» dit-elle. «Je ne demande qu'un verre d'eau.»

Finalmente llegó a una plaza grande. La gente estaba sentada alrededor de mesas sombreadas por árboles, charlando y riendo. Bajo una inmensa sombrilla, había unos camareros parados tras un mostrador, que estaban sirviendo bebidas frías en vasos altos y escarchados. En este momento la sirena se dio cuenta de lo cansada y sedienta que estaba. Sabía que un trago de agua la reviviría. Pero cuando se acercó al mostrador y pidió agua, el camarero le extendió la mano.

—No tengo dinero —dijo ella—. Lo único que quiero es un vaso con agua.

The waiter shook his head firmly.

"We have only bottled mineral water, and it is for sale, not free. Besides, you cannot occupy a table here without ordering something." His tone of voice sent her back into the street.

This, of course, was a big disappointment to the mermaid, who had yearned so much to mingle with human beings. Instead, she wandered about town, looking into store windows, and saw a sea of price tags. Clothes, shoes, jewelry, books, toys. . . everything had its price. Humans need money to be happy, the mermaid realized. And

Doch der Kellner schüttelte unerbittlich den Kopf.

"Wir führen nur Mineralwasser in Flaschen und zwar zum Verkaufen, nicht umsonst. Du kannst auch nicht hier am Tisch sitzen, ohne etwas zu bestellen." Sein unwirscher Ton wies sie zurück auf die Strasse.

Das war natürlich eine grosse Enttäuschung für die Nixe, die sich so viel von den Menschen erhofft hatte. Sie irrte in der Stadt umher, schaute in die Auslagen und sah ein Meer von Preiszetteln. Kleider, Schuhe, Schmuck, Bücher, Spielzeug - alles hatte seinen Preis. "Die Menschen brauchen Geld zum Glücklichsein", stellte die Nixe

Le garçon secoua fermement la tête.

«Nous n'avons que de l'eau minérale en bouteille, et on la vend, elle n'est pas gratuite. Ici, vous ne pouvez pas non plus occuper une table sans rien commander.» Au ton désagréable de sa voix, elle repartit dans la rue.

Tout cela, bien sûr, était très décevant pour la sirène qui avait tant souhaité se mêler aux êtres humains. Alors, elle déambula dans la ville, regardant les vitrines des magasins, et vit une marée d'étiquettes de prix. Vêtements, chaussures, bijoux, livres, jouets...tout avait un prix. Les êtres humains ont besoin d'argent pour être heureux, se dit

El camarero sacudió la cabeza firmemente. —Sólo tenemos agua mineral embotellada, y está a la venta, no es gratis. Aquí no puedes ocupar una mesa sin ordenar algo. —Su tono de voz la lanzó de vuelta a la calle.

Esto, por supuesto, fue una gran desilusión para la sirena, que tanto había anhelado mezclarse con los seres humanos. En vez de ello, anduvo errando por el pueblo, mirando los escaparates de las tiendas y vio un mar de etiquetas de precio. Vestidos, zapatos, joyas, libros, juguetes... todo tenía su precio. Los humanos necesitan dinero para

because they must buy their pleasures, when they have no money, they are far lonelier than I am.

As the mermaid again made her way past the crowded square, a familiar cry suddenly filled her ears. She whirled around. At one of the tables someone had tipped over a glass of water. A well-dressed woman was trying to brush the water form her skirt with a napkin. The mermaid recognized her instantly, it was the woman she had seen sunbathing on the rubber float in the pool.

At the sight of her the mermaid turned her head, fearing the woman would recognize her. Then it dawned

fest. "Sie kaufen sich ihr Vergnügen, doch besitzen sie einmal kein Geld, so sind sie noch viel einsamer als ich."

Als die Nixe sich wieder ihren Weg über den belebten Platz bahnte, da hörte sie plötzlich ein vertrautes Kreischen. Sie fuhr herum. An einem der Tische hatte man ein Glas umgestossen. Eine gut gekleidete Frau versuchte aufgeregt, mit der Serviette das Wasser von ihrem Rock zu wischen. Die Nixe erkannte sie sofort; es war die Frau, die sich im Schwimmbad auf der Matratze gesonnt hatte.

Bei ihrem Anblick wandte die Nixe den Kopf ab, aus Furcht, von der Frau erkannt zu werden. Doch dann

la sirène. Et comme ils paient pour leurs plaisirs, quand ils n'ont pas d'argent, ils sont encore plus seuls que moi.

Comme la sirène fendait à nouveau la foule du square, un son familier parvint soudain à ses oreilles. Elle se retourna. A une table, quelqu'un avait renversé un verre d'eau. Une dame bien habillée essayait d'éponger l'eau sur sa jupe avec une serviette. La sirène la reconnut immédiatement, c'était la dame qu'elle avait vue en train de prendre un bain de soleil sur le matelas pneumatique dans la piscine.

En la voyant, la sirène se détourna, craignant que la dame ne la reconnût. Puis elle se dit: «Comment peut-elle

ser felices, comprendió la sirena. Y como compran sus placeres, cuando carecen de dinero, están mucho más solos que yo.

Mientras la sirena se abría paso a través de la plaza congestionada, repentinamente oyó un sonido que le era familiar. Se dio la vuelta. En una de las mesas alguien había derramado un vaso de agua. Una mujer bien vestida estaba tratando de limpiar el agua de su falda con una servilleta. La sirena la reconoció instantáneamente, era la mujer que había visto en la piscina asoleándose sobre el flotador de goma.

En cuanto la vio, la sirena volteó la cara, temerosa de que la mujer la reconociera. Entonces comprendió;

on her; how can she recognize me if she's never seen me? The next moment something else came to her mind. Her thoughts went to the crawling infant, alone in the garden, and she began to grow uneasy.

Suddenly, the merman's angry shouts rang in her ears, "No sense of responsibility! Good for nothing!" Those had been his words when he left her, feeling wounded and resentful, in the pool. But hadn't he been right? She had thought only of herself and her loneliness and had totally forgotten her task.

überlegte sie: "Wie soll sie mich erkennen, da sie mich noch nie gesehen hat?" Aber noch etwas anderes kam ihr in den Sinn. Ihr fiel das herumkriechende Baby ein, allein im Garten, und ihr wurde ganz ängstlich zumute.

Plötzlich erinnerte sie sich auch der Worte des zornigen Wassermanns: "Kein Verantwortungsbewusstsein! Zu nichts zu gebrauchen!" Das waren seine Worte gewesen, damals, als er sie beleidigt und unzufrieden in ihrem Becken zurückgelassen hatte. Doch musste sie ihm nicht recht geben? Sie hatte nur an sich und ihre Einsamkeit gedacht und darüber ganz ihre Aufgabe vergessen.

me reconnaître puisqu'elle ne m'a jamais vue?» L'instant d'après, une autre chose lui vint à l'esprit. Ses pensées se portèrent vers le petit enfant, qui ne pouvait que ramper, qui était seul dans le jardin, et elle commença à se sentir mal à l'aise.

Soudain, les propos coléreux du triton retentirent dans sa tête: «Aucun sens des responsabilités! Bonne à rien!» Tels avaient été les mots qu'il avait employés quand il l'avait laissée, blessée et mécontente, dans la piscine. Mais n'avait-il pas eu raison? Elle n'avait pensé qu'à elle-même et à sa solitude, et avait complètement oublié sa tâche.

—cómo puede reconocerme si jamás me ha visto? —En ese instante, algo más le vino a la mente. Sus pensamiento se dirigieron al bebé que gateaba, solo en el jardín, y empezó a inquietarse.

De pronto, los gritos coléricos del tritón retumbaron en sus oídos: «¡Ningún sentido de responsabilidad! ¡Buena para nada!» Esas habían sido sus palabras al dejarla, sintiéndose herida y resentida, en la piscina. Acaso no había estado él en lo correcto? Ella sólo había pensado en sí misma y en su soledad, olvidando su tarea por completo.

She realized that an even more severe scolding awaited her when the merman learned of her newest escapade. But, at the moment, this was less of a concern to her than her worry about the child.

The mermaid looked anxiously about the square, but saw no one whom she could ask for help. Suddenly she spotted the large stone sculpture rising from the fountain in the middle of the square. Two dragons were spraying jets of water upon the god of the sea while a mermaid handed him a stone bowl to drink from.

Es war ihr klar, dass sie eine Strafpredigt zu erwarten hatte, sobald der Wassermann von ihrem Ausflug erfuhr. Doch bedrückte sie dies im Augenblick weniger, als die lähmende Sorge um das Kind.

Die Nixe blickte hilfesuchend um sich, fand aber niemanden, den sie um Beistand bitten konnte. Ihr Auge blieb an einer Steingruppe haften, die mitten auf dem Platz aus einem Springbrunnen aufragte. Zwei wasserspeiende Drachen benetzten den Gott des Meeres, während eine Seejungfrau ihm eine Schale zum Trinken reichte.

Elle se rendit compte qu'une réprimande encore plus sévère l'attendait quand le triton apprendrait sa nouvelle escapade. Mais pour l'instant, ceci la préoccupait moins que son inquiétude au sujet de l'enfant.

La sirène regarda avec anxiété autour d'elle mais ne vit personne à qui elle pût demander de l'aide. Soudain, elle aperçut la grande sculpture de pierre qui s'élevait dans la fontaine, au milieu du square. Deux dragons lançaient des jets d'eau au-dessus du dieu de la mer tandis qu'une sirène lui tendait un vase de pierre pour y boire.

Se dió cuenta de que le esperaba una reprimenda aún más severa cuando el tritón se enterara de su reciente escapada. No obstante, de momento, esto la angustiaba menos que su preocupación por el niño.

La sirena buscó ansiosamente en la plaza, sin encontrar a quién pedirle ayuda. Finalmente, detectó la escultura hecha de una gran piedra sobre la fuente situada en medio de la plaza. Dos dragones escupían chorros de agua sobre el dios del mar mientras una sirena le extendía un tazón de piedra para beber.

The mermaid hurried toward the fountain. Impatiently she tugged at the buttons of her robe, threw off the garment and jumped into the fountain. With both arms she clasped the figure of the god, and tears ran down her cheeks as she implored, "O' great spirit of the water, please help me. Send me back to the pool and let me perform the task given to me. I accept what punishment I deserve, but help me find my way back to my place."

While she was pleading fervently, dark clouds had arisen. A stiff wind sprang up and whirled umbrellas, tablecloths and newspapers about. The people in the

Die Nixe lief auf den Brunnen zu. Ungeduldig riss sie an den Knöpfen des Rockes, warf das Kleidungsstück ab und sprang mit einem Satz in den Brunnen. Mit beiden Armen umklammerte sie die Götterfigur, während dicke Tränen über ihre Wangen rollten. "Alle guten Geister des Wassers, helft mir", flehte sie. "Bringt mich zurück zu meinem Becken, und lasst mich die Aufgabe erfüllen, die mir gestellt war. Jede Strafe nehme ich auf mich, nur lasst mich zurückfinden zu meinem Platz."

Während sie inbrünstig betete, waren dunkle Wolken aufgezogen. Ein heftiger Wind war aufgekommen und wirbelte Sonnenschirme, Tischtücher und Zeitungen durcheinander. Die Menschen begannen in alle Richtungen

La sirène se hâta vers la fontaine. Elle tira impatiemment sur les boutons de son peignoir, jeta le vêtement par terre et sauta dans la fontaine. De ses deux bras, elle étreignit la sculpture du dieu, et les larmes se mirent à couler sur ses joues tandis qu'elle implorait: «Oh, grand esprit des eaux, aide-moi, s'il te plaît! Renvoie-moi vers la piscine et laisse-moi accomplir la tâche qui m'a été confiée. J'accepte la punition que je mérite, mais aide-moi à retrouver le chemin de ma demeure.»

Pendant qu'elle priait avec ferveur, de sombres nuages étaient apparus, un vent fort s'était levé et faisait tourbillonner parasols, nappes et journaux. Les gens dans les

La sirena se apresuró hacia la fuente. Impacientemente, tiró con fuerza de los botones de la bata, desechó la vestimenta y saltó en la fuente. Con ambos brazos, apretó la figura del dios, y le imploró con lágrimas cayendo sobre sus mejillas: —Oh, gran espíritu del agua, por favor ayúdame. Envíame de regreso a la piscina y permíteme realizar la tarea que se me ha dado. Acepto el castigo que merezco, pero ayúdame a encontrar el camino de regreso a mi sitio.

Mientras que ella rogaba fervientemente, empezaron a surgir nubes obscuras. De repente, un fuerte viento se levantó, volteando paraguas, manteles y periódicos. La

streets began to scatter in every direction.

"A thunderstorm!" someone shouted. "Take cover, quick!"

The waiters scurried to clear the tables as fast as they could. The ice-cream vendor rolled his cart away, and the newspaper stand was wrapped with a watertight canvas. In almost no time the square was empty.

But still clinging tightly to the stone statue, the mermaid noticed none of this. Only when the first big drops of rain splashed on her shoulders did she begin to recover.

davonzulaufen.

"Ein Gewitter!" schrie jemand. "Schnell, stellt euch unter!"

Die Kellner versuchten in Windeseile, die Tische abzuräumen. Der Eisverkäufer rollte seinen Wagen vom Platz, und der Zeitungsstand wurde mit einer wasserdichten Plache überzogen. In Kürze war der Platz menschenleer.

Immer noch zu Füssen der Götterfigur, bemerkte die Nixe von all dem nichts. Erst als die ersten grossen Tropfen platschend auf ihre Schultern fielen, kam sie wieder zu

rues se dispersèrent dans toutes les directions.

«Voilà l'orage!» cria quelqu'un. «Abritez-vous vite!»

Les garçons de café se précipitèrent pour débarrasser les tables aussi rapidement que possible. Le vendeur de glaces partit en poussant son chariot et le kiosque à journaux fut recouvert d'une bâche imperméable. En un rien de temps, le square fut vide.

Toujours cramponnée à la statue de pierre, la sirène ne remarqua rien de tout cela. Ce fut seulement lorsque les premières grosses gouttes de pluie éclaboussèrent ses épaules qu'elle reprit peu á peu ses esprits. Rapidement,

gente empezó a dispersarse en todas las direcciones.

—¡Una tormenta! —alguien gritó—. ¡Cúbranse, pronto!

Los camareros se escabulleron para limpiar las mesas lo más rápido posible. El vendedor de helados se llevó su carrito, y el puesto de periódicos fué cubierto con una lona impermeable. Casi de inmediato la plaza quedó vacía.

La sirena no se percató de nada de esto, pues aún estaba pegada fuertemente a la estatua de piedra. Sólo cuando las primeras grandes gotas de lluvia salpicaron sobre sus hombres, se empezó a recuperar. Pronto los

Soon the torrents of rain came down all around her, and the mermaid was envelope by her element. What pleasure she felt, being able to move about freely again.

She half floated, half climbed up into the pouring rain, as if on a staircase, over the roofs, back to the friendly, quiet street she had come from. But how would she recognize the garden, she wondered.

Nearly all of the houses she saw had swimming pools, and most of the gardens had palm trees whose leaves were reflected in the water. But in only one of these gardens was

sich. Bald stürzte der Regen in Strömen zu Boden, und die Nixe war von ihrem Element umgeben. Was für ein Vergnügen es für sie war, sich wieder gelöst bewegen zu können.

Halb schwamm sie, halb stieg sie im Regen wie auf einer Treppe empor, über die Dächer hinweg, der freundlichen Strasse entgegen. Wie würde sie aber ihren Garten erkennen? fragte sie sich.

Fast alle Häuser, die sie sah, besassen ein Schwimmbad, und in den meisten Gärten standen Palmen, deren Blätter sich im Wasser spiegelten. Doch nur in einem ein-

des torrents d'eau s'abattirent tout autour d'elle, et elle se trouva enveloppée dans son élément. Grand fut son plaisir de pouvoir à nouveau se mouvoir librement.

A moitié flottant, à moitié grimpant dans la pluie drue, comme sur un escalier, elle s'éleva au-dessus des toits, et retourna vers la rue calme et familière d'où elle était venue. Mais comment reconnaître le jardin, se demandait-elle.

Presque toutes les maisons qu'elle voyait avaient des piscines, et la plupart des jardins avaient des palmiers dont les feuilles se reflétaient dans l'eau. Mais c'était dans un

torrentes de lluvia descendieron por todo su alrededor, y la sirena se quedó envuelta en su elemento. ¡Qué placer sentía, poder moverse libremente otra vez!

Flotando a medias, ella se abrió paso por la pesada lluvia y, como subiendo una escalera, atravesó los tejados, para regresar a la calle amistosa y tranquila de donde había venido. Pero, ¿como iba a reconocer el jardín? se preguntó.

Casi todas las casas que vio tenían piscina, y casi todos los jardines tenían palmeras cuyas hojas se reflejaban en el agua. Pero sólo en uno de esos jardines había un viejo

standing an old red setter, looking completely drenched, his ears dripping water as he sniffed the rim of the pool as though searching for something lost.

"I'm coming, wait for me!" shouted the mermaid from high above. Then she mounted a cascade of raindrops and started to slide down on them as if on a chute, directly into the pool. She landed with an enormous splash, soaking the dog from nose to tail. He began to howl, to bark wildly and danced on his hind legs as though filled with elation.

zigen Garten stand ein alter, roter Setter, völlig durchnässt, mit triefenden Ohren, und schnüffelte unglücklich am Beckenrand, als hätte er etwas verloren.

"Ich komme schon, warte auf mich!" rief die Nixe von ganz hoch oben. Dann setzte sie sich auf die Regentropfen und begann wie auf einer Rutsche hinunterzusausen, direkt hinein in das Becken. Sie landete mit einem riesigen Platsch und bespritzte den Hund von oben bis unten. Der aber begann zu jaulen, zu bellen, und tanzte vor lauter Freude auf den Hinterpfoten.

seul de ces jardins que se trouvait un vieux setter roux, complètement trempé, les oreilles dégoulinantes d'eau, qui flairait tout autour de la piscine comme s'il cherchait quelque chose de perdu.

«J'arrive, attends-moi!» cria la sirène d'en haut. Elle se jucha au sommet d'une cascade de pluie et se laissa glisser comme sur une chute d'eau, directement dans la piscine. Elle atterrit avec un énorme plongeon, arrosant le chien du museau à la queue. Il se mit à hurler, à aboyer frénétiquement et à danser sur ses pattes arrière, plein d'allégresse.

setter pelirrojo, que estaba totalmente empapado, con las orejas escurriendo mientras olfateaba la orilla de la piscina como en busca de algo perdido.

—¡Ya vengo, espérame! —gritó la sirena desde muy alto. Entonces ella se montó sobre una cascada de gotas de lluvia y empezó a deslizarse en ellas hacia abajo como si fueran un paracaídas, metiéndose en la piscina. Cayó salpicando enormemente, empapando al perro de la nariz hasta el rabo. El empezó a aullar, a ladrar frenéticamente y a danzar sobre sus patas traseras como si estuviera lleno de regocijo.

Just then the rain let up. The dark clouds began to part. A small patch of blue sky suddenly peeked through and a yellow ray of sunshine crept across the garden.

As if on cue, the baby came crawling out of the house like a little turtle. He gazed in wonderment at the wet world all around him. The stalks of grass were moist with raindrops, and so were the flowers and the rocks. As he crawled across the garden, his hands also grew wet. So did his cheeks. Filled with curiosity the baby bent over the pool. Would the water be wet, too?

Nun liess der Regen nach. Die dunklen Wolken zogen auseinander. Ein schmaler Streifen blauen Himmels wurde wieder sichtbar, und ein Sonnenstrahl fiel in den Garten.

Das Kind kam aus dem Haus gekrochen wie eine kleine Schildkröte. Erstaunt blickte es auf die nasse Welt. Die Grashalme waren nass, die Blumen und die Steine. Selbst seine eigenen Hände wurden nass, während es durch den Garten kroch, und ebenso seine Wangen. Neugierig beugte das Kind sich über das Becken. Ob das Wasser wohl auch nass war?

Juste à ce moment là, la pluie cessa. Les nuages sombres commençèrent à s'écarter. Un petit coin de ciel bleu apparut et un rayon de soleil doré se coula dans le jardin.

Comme s'il répondait à un signal, l'enfant sortit de la maison en rampant, tel une petite tortue. Il découvrait avec émerveillement le monde humide qui l'entourait. Les brins d'herbe étaient mouillés par les gouttes de pluie, de même que les fleurs et les cailloux. En rampant à travers le jardin, ses mains aussi se mouillèrent, ainsi que ses joues. Rempli de curiosité, l'enfant se pencha au bord de la piscine. L'eau était-elle mouillée aussi?

Justo entonces, cesó la lluvia. Las nubes obscuras empezaron a irse. Una pequeña mancha de cielo azul se asomó repentinamente y un rayo de sol amarillo se extendió por el jardín.

Como respondiendo a una señal, el bebé salió de la casa gateando del mismo modo que una pequeña tortuga, y contempló con asombro el mundo húmedo que le rodeaba. Los pedúnculos de pasto estaban húmedos debido a las gotas de lluvia, al igual que las flores y las rocas. Al cruzar el jardín gateando, sus manos y sus mejillas también se humedecieron. Lleno de curiosidad, el bebé se inclinó hacia la piscina. ¿Estará el agua húmeda, tambien?

The child leaned forward, straining to touch the glassy surface. Just then he lost his balance and fell into the pool head first, right into the outstretched arms of the mermaid.

The baby felt heavy to her, surprisingly heavy for one so small, but also surprisingly lovable. Never before had the mermaid seen a human being so close up. The finely-drawn eyebrows, the large, round eyes that looked at her in uncomprehending amazement. Quickly, she raised the baby up above the water so his little mouth could gasp for air. She held him firmly and securely.

Das Kind beugte sich vor und versuchte, die spiegelnde Fläche zu berühren. Da verlor es das Gleichgewicht und fiel kopfüber in das Bad, direkt in die Arme der Nixe.

Schwer kam ihr das Baby vor, erstaunlich schwer für einen so kleinen Körper, doch andererseits so liebenswert. Noch nie hatte die Nixe ein menschliches Wesen von so nahe gesehen. Die feingezeichneten Brauen, die grossen, runden Augen, die sie in fassungslosem Staunen anblickten. Schnell hielt sie das Kind über Wasser, so dass der kleine Mund nach Luft schnappen konnte. Sie hielt es sicher und fest.

L'enfant se pencha en avant, s'efforçant de toucher la surface miroitante. C'est alors qu'il perdit l'équilibre et tomba dans la piscine la tête la première, droit dans les bras tendus de la sirène.

L'enfant lui parut lourd, étonnamment lourd pour quelqu'un de si petit, mais aussi étonnamment adorable. Jamais auparavant la sirène n'avait vu un être humain d'aussi près. Les sourcils finement dessinés, les grands yeux tout ronds qui la regardaient avec un mélange de stupeur et d'incompréhension. Elle souleva vivement l'enfant au-dessus de l'eau pour que sa petite bouche pût aspirer de l'air. Elle le tenait fermement et avec sûreté.

El niño se inclinó hacia adelante, esforzándose por tocar la superficie vidriosa. Justo entonces, perdió el equilibrio y cayó de cabeza en la piscina, pero exactamente en los brazos extendidos de la sirena.

Ella sintió al bebé pesado, sorprendentemente pesado para ser tan pequeño, pero también sorprendentemente adorable. La sirena nunca había visto antes tan cerca a un ser humano. Las cejas trazadas finamente, los ojos largos y redondos que la veían con asombro incomprensible. Rápidamente, ella sacó al bebé del agua para que su boca diminuta pudiera inhalar aire. Lo mantuvo firmemente y a salvo.

Just then, the nanny came rushing from the house. Seeing the child floating on the water, she dashed frantically toward him, pulled him out of the pool and screamed so loudly that neighbors came running from every direction. They shook the child, patting him on the back until he started to cry. The nanny sobbed, the child bawled, the dog barked, and the neighbors, struggling to make themselves heard, all shouted louder than one another. These were the same nerve-wracking noises the mermaid had disliked so much, but now they were almost music to her ears.

Da kam das Kindermädchen aus dem Haus gelaufen. Als sie das Kind im Wasser sah, stürzte sie herzu, zog es aus dem Becken und schrie so laut, dass die ganze Nachbarschaft angelaufen kam. Man schüttelte das Kind und klopfte ihm auf den Rücken, bis es zu weinen begann. Das Kindermädchen schluchzte, das Kind plärrte, der Hund bellte, und alle Nachbarn versuchten einander zu überschreien, um sich bemerkbar zu machen. Es waren dieselben lästigen Geräusche, die die Nixe so sehr verabscheut hatte, nun aber klangen sie fast wie Musik in ihren Ohren.

À ce moment là, la gouvernante sortit précipitamment de la maison. Voyant l'enfant flotter sur l'eau, elle se rua frénétiquement vers lui, le tira hors de la piscine et cria si fort que les voisins arrivèrent de partout en courant. Ils secouèrent l'enfant, lui tapotant le dos jusqu'à ce qu'il se mît à pleurer. La gouvernante sanglotait, l'enfant braillait, le chien aboyait, et les voisins, rivalisant pour se faire entendre, criaient tous plus fort les uns que les autres. C'étaient là les mêmes bruits exaspérants que la sirène avait tant détestés, mais maintenant ils étaient presque comme de la musique à ses oreilles.

Justo entonces, la niñera se aproximó con urgencia desde la casa. Al ver al chico flotando sobre el agua, se abalanzó frenéticamente hacia él, lo sacó de la piscina y gritó tan fuerte que los vecinos vinieron corriendo de todos lados. Sacudieron al niño, dándole palmadas en la espalda hasta que empezó a chillar. La muchacha sollozó, el chico berreó, el perro ladró, y los vecinos, con dificultad, se pusieron a gritar para hacerse oír. Estos eran los mismos ruidos enervantes que tanto le disgustaban a la sirena, pero ahora eran casi como música para sus oídos.

Though she could barely move, her tail was sore from the day's long outing and her arms ached with exertion, the mermaid felt happier than at any time she could remember.

"Thank you," she murmured quietly to the force of Nature. "I am so grateful to you for what you have taught me today. Now I realize that only by doing what is expected of me can I find meaning and purpose in life."

Content at last, she let herself glide to the bottom of the pool, then folded her arms serenely and dreamed of a merman.

Zwar konnte sie sich kaum rühren, ihre Flosse war wund von dem langen Marschieren, und ihre Arme schmerzten von der Anstrengung, doch war die Nixe so glücklich wie nie zuvor in ihrem Leben.

"Danke", flüsterte sie den geheimen Kräften der Natur zu. "Ich bin so dankbar für das, was ihr mich heute gelehrt habt. Erst jetzt verstehe ich, dass man seinem Leben selbst Bedeutung geben muss, indem man die Aufgaben erfüllt, die einem gestellt werden."

Befriedigt liess sie sich an der tiefsten Stelle des Beckens zu Boden sinken, verschränkte die Arme über ihrem Körper und träumte von einem Wassermann.

Bien qu'elle pût à peine bouger, sa queue étant endolorie par la longue sortie de la journée, et ses bras brisés par l'effort, la sirène se sentit plus heureuse qu'elle ne l'avait jamais été.

«Merci» murmura-t-elle doucement aux forces de la Nature. «Je vous suis reconnaissante pour ce que vous m'avez enseigné aujourd'hui. Maintenant je me rends compte que c'est seulement en faisant ce que l'on attend de moi que je peux trouver un sens et un but à ma vie.»

Enfin satisfaite, elle se laissa glisser au fond de la piscine, replia sereinement les bras et se mit à rêver d'un triton.

Aunque apenas podía moverse, su cola estaba inflamada debido a la larga excursión del día y sus brazos doloridos por tanto esfuerzo, la sirena se sentía más feliz que en ningún otro momento que pudiera recordar.

—Gracias, —susurró a las fuerzas de la Naturaleza—. Estoy tan agradecida con ustedes por lo que hoy me han enseñado. Ahora me percato de que, sólo haciendo lo que se espera de mí puedo encontrar significado y finalidad en la vida.

Contenta al fin, se deslizó al fondo de la piscina, cruzó los brazos serenamente y empezó a soñar con un tritón.